POETRY THROUGH THE *Eyes* OF MY *Soul*

ARNOLD SHURN

authorHOUSE®

AuthorHouse™
1663 Liberty Drive
Bloomington, IN 47403
www.authorhouse.com
Phone: 1 (800) 839-8640

Published by AuthorHouse 01/07/2019

ISBN: 978-1-5462-6378-4 (sc)
ISBN: 978-1-5462-6379-1 (hc)
ISBN: 978-1-5462-6377-7 (e)

Library of Congress Control Number: 2018912309

Print information available on the last page.

This book is printed on acid-free paper.

Introduction

I was given life and God transferred that energy to Herbert L. Shurn and Theresa Jackson Nichols Shurn. I was born and raised in Cleveland, Ohio off of St.Clair Ave. During my short existence here on earth I have witnessed many atrocities, but I have seen an enormous amount of joy also.

My initial thoughts were to express the social ills endured by the downtrodden of society. However, I decided to express my life experiences. Therefore, my poems are expression through the eyes of my soul.

~I dedicate this book to my nephew BIG MIKE my four brothers, my mother and all the others. This is for all my family and friends. Love you all RIP!

MOST IMPORANTLY, I WANTED TO REVEAL TO THE READERS TO ALWAYS BE CRITICAL THINKERS. THE WORLD WE WE LIVE IN IS NOT ALWAYS TRANSLUCENT, SO LOOK BEYOUND THE TELEVISION SOUND BITES, AND THE HALF TRUTHS, AND SEEK THE NAKED TRUTHS, LOOK AT LIFE THROUGH THE EYES OF YOUR SOUL, AND SEEK THE PEACE THAT IS WITH IN.

XI

For more information contact: shurn.arnold@yahoo.com/ Face book/ Arnold Shurn/

Contents

Mama Sleep

Mama sleeps and awakens no more to the sorrows of this world.
Mama sleeps and awakens no more to the cruelties
Heartaches, pains and the evils of this world.
Mama sleep you have raised boys into men,
And touched the lives of countless friends.
Mama you was a dedicated wife and raised four beautiful girls
What a wonderful blessing you were to this world

This a day of joy not sorrow,
Because I know in my heart
I will see you tomorrow.
For this day you are now free,
And forever will your loving spirit
Dwell inside of me.

Mama I have no more tears to cry today,
Because I know the almighty in his own infinite wisdom has made for you a better way.
This day must be done,
Because I realize that we all will have our day in the sun
Mama sleeps and awakens no more to the pain and sorrows of this world.
My promises I will keep,
so mama sleep.
Mama the criterion to enter heaven is love,
then rest assure that the pearly gates await you up above.
Mama sleep in your angelical sleep,
For you have ran your race,
With amazing grace

Mama Sleep.
In loving memory of my dear mother
May 2, 2004

Mommy Please Stop Yelling at me

Mommy it is not my fault your life turned out to be the way it is,
so mommy please stop yelling at me
Mommy it was you who chose to do drugs instead of getting an education
Mommy I did not ask to be born out of wedlock,
So Mommy please stop yelling at me
.

Mama it is your responsibility to love and nurture me
Mama stop blaming me for having babies,
You knew darn well you couldn't support us

Mama, quit calling me dumb, stupid, and telling me I'll never be anything
It is not my fault, now you are angry at me
Mama you had a choice to be or do anything you wanted,
I did not have a choice in the matter of who my parents were going to be,
So please give me a chance to be all I can be,

Mama please stop blaming me for your mistakes in life,
And give me a chance to have a productive life
Let me soar, let me fly,
And let me have a chance at this thing called life.
I did not have a choice, so mama stop yelling at me!

-For the children who have suffered mental abuse from their parent's 2003.

Sisters in locks

India Arie said," that you are not your hair",
So my sister's you shouldn't care when they stop to stare,
And criticize your beautiful nappy hair.
You must de-program that Eurocentric view,
And learn to love you.
My dark, My caramel, My Creole, My, light complexion vanilla sister's.
My sister's you are the original creation of life.
Sister's do you know, that all life came from you?
My sister's, stop polluting your beautiful body with all these chemicals just so you can have an unnatural look,
And stop spending your hard earned dollars, out of your pocket book,
Just to have that Barbie doll look
Take a page out of your own Afro – Centric book,
And wear that natural look.
My sister's it is your duty,
As the original woman to carry your own natural beauty
Do you remember when you were told that your natural beauty was evil?
And that your full lips were ugly, and your big fat butt was too big and round,
And that your hair was scary
Take a good look around because you've got those same folks,
Who brain washed you into thinking that your natural beauty was horrific,
They're now trying to steal your hips, lips, and your behind.
They even got you believing that you're inferior to their kind.

Sister's stop following the signs of time,
And utilize your own mind.
Sister's you are the greatest creation ever put upon this earth,
So wear that blackness for all the world to see
Because your natural hair is beautiful, and it's free.

April 11, 2004

Son

My dear son when I had you I was young.

I never saw your first walk or even your first talk.

I'm not going to play the blame game, because I had a choice.

I would call but wouldn't' get the chance to hear your voice.

I became angry, mad, and sad.

I gave up the plight when all I ever wanted was to be a dad.

I should have stayed to fight,

but instead I threw up my hand.

I should have fought for my rights.

Now I feel less than a man,

Because I should have stayed and fought,

And should have done all that I can .

I wouldn't be having sad thoughts,

I could have won,

The rights to share these lost words

I love you son.

~Just crying out for the love of my son~
December 9, 20005

I Love You

I love you because of who you are

And right from the start

You looked at my heart

You looked far beyond my exterior

And through love you examined my interior.

You brought out things in me that I never knew.

You make my heart dance when I think of you

You are like the water to a seed you make me grow

And with every passing day I love you more and more

For this is love and this I know.

When my back was against the wall,

It was you who encouraged me to hold my head up and stand tall.

When I no longer could take what this life bear,

I just think of your love because I know its there.

My love I am going to keep it short but real,

And tell you exactly how I feel.

MY words I say are true,

And in this poem I simply saying I love you.--*May 12, 2004*

Pain

If I could take your pain and change its name, I would

If I could take all my love and heal your pain, I would.

If I could make your darkness turn into light, I would.

If I could find the right words to comfort your broken heart, I would.

Life's experience has shown me that pain won't last for always.

If I could take your pain away, for a moment, or just for a day, I would.

I even wish I could make it go away.

Since I can't make your pain go away, I simply will say.

I love you each and every day.

-A person that I knew was telling me about their problems and I felt so defenseless.
December 26, 2002

Can I get paid?

I don't mean to make no fuss, but this job got my life all messed up it's like I am still riding on the back of the bus
This job got my life in an uproar, because I'm tired of being classified as the working poor
. If I'm going to go to work and still be poor;
Then what the heck am I working for.
And the more they decide to take.
People when are we going to get our tax break?
I go to work everyday and I still can't gain any wealth,
And beside they don't even want to pay for my health.
Brothers this job got my life in a wreck,
because I'm just like all the rest of the 46 million
Uninsured I'm living pay check to pay check.
I've been in the cheese lines, welfare lines, and unemployment line
, and now they got me standing in the check cashing advance line.
Gas prices are sky high and I can barely getting by.
Maybe this is why my brothers and sisters turn to dope
, because they just don't see any hope.
People its time for us to come to the realization that were all in the same boat,
And we're hanging on by a very very thin rope.
We're all trying to live that American dream by working that 9 to 5, but we're barely staying alive,
And my j. o.b. is keeps me just over broke.
I got a job,
but on pay day, it seems like I'm being strong armed robbed.
Brothers this job got my life in a wreck,
I'm tired of living pay check to pay check.
And in the words of Fanny Lou Hammer I'm sick of tired of being sick and tired....of being sick of being sick and tired.
Oh well, let me go to work so I can get a pay check.

-August 19, 2005

Strong Black Man

I've been beaten, lied to and stolen from my mother land.
But, yet I still stand as a strong Blackman.
I've had to helplessly watch them rape my mothers, sisters, fathers and my brothers.
I've survived their attempted genocide and terrorist acts.
I have survived their unemployment system, welfare system, and their "just-us" system.
I've had to carry the weight of unspeakable atrocities on my back just because I'm black.
I ask what other humans have endured the rapping of his history,
Wealth, name and still remain psychologically sane?
It was my blood and sweat from my unpaid hands that build this Ameri-can.
That's why I will continue to walk with my head up,
Because I ain't never ever giving up.
And through it all,
I'm still standing tall,
I am a strong Blackman.
Always striving to be the best that I can,
Because I am America, so I can.
I am the mighty and strong Black man

Holy Tree

This is not a religious sale, but I do have my story to tell.
We must start loving our fellowman regardless of our religious plan
If we don't then we're all headed on a collision course to hell
Why destroy humanity with this religious discrimination?
People we can all live happy, joyous, and free
because we are not separate like leaves,
we are branches from the Holy Tree.
if we are all created by one God, then that make us sisters and brothers,
and didn't God say love one another?
Why should it matter what religion we claim,
Because it's only a name
Hinduism, Buddhism, Confucianism, Islam, Judaism, or Christianity,
If all religions are based on love, so why do we hate, and act out this inhumanity?
When all God asked was to love and create a better humanity.
Only if we could see, we could see that we are all branches
From God's Holy Tree
People let's start loving one another so we can live happy, joyous and free,
Because your religion don't make you better than me
People stop using religion to hate,
Can we start loving under one faith?
And call it the human race.
Take the blinders off, and we will live happy, joyous and free,
Under Gods Holy Tree.

Am I A Poet?

Am I a poet? I've never placed first, second, or third
And the only thing the audience received was an opportunity to hear my spoken words
Now don't get me wrong. I would love to win every now and then,
but they say my words are invisible like the wind
and that that I don't have the stuff to win..
But I've learned through the process of opinions,
and that is everybody got an opinion.

And who to say whose opinions is right or wrong,
Because after all it's just an opinion.
And your opinions are like Bush and Gore,
They don't count no more.
So if I don't win and place fourth again,
I've learned that your opinions,
Don't count no more.

I'm not going to allow anyone to put my words on a shelf,
Because I love this spoken word but most of all I love myself.
So take your opinions and shove up your opinionated….
.I'm not going to curse but it rhymes with
The word that describes me called class.
Just cause I don't huff and puff or talk real loud,
But what I got to say will touch the crowd.
I'm not going to talk about having a revolution,
But I'll offer a positive solution.
I don't grab my genitals or call my sister's animals,
I do respect me and my queens
I've been told that black queen stuff is getting pretty old.
I am not trying to cling to no bling bling or have a one night fling.
Well if my words are getting old because I choose to respect my black queen,
Take your opinions because they don't mean a thing

And if I don't place first, second, or third, then give me my usual fourth place,
And like always, I will smile and walk away with grace,
Because in my heart I still got my self-esteem,
And I am living my dream,
My opinion the one that counts the most,
Because I am still a winner

—I'm still a winner. 12/13/04

Just a Friend

I've always done what a real man supposed to do,
But I guess my love wasn't good enough for you
After all this time, you tell me that I'm not man enough for you
Baby, I've always tried to be good to you and for you.
Now you want to go and break my heart in two
Baby, please tell me why I wasn't man enough for you.
That's a lie about a man isn't supposed to cry,
Because when you broke my heart that's all I did was cry.
Baby, please tell me what can I do? I can't eat, I can't sleep, baby what about the times
When you said, "you love me."
I guess those words didn't really mean a thing.
Damn girl, I was ready to buy that diamond ring.
Baby you gave me your precious body but not your heart
But please help me heal my broken heart,
Baby help me find a brand new start.
And what's with this new terminology in today's relationships,
Because women are now using the term he's just a friend,
I believe once you let a brother all the way in.
We became more than just a friend.
Women are acting more and more like these dog a** men,
With this new sh** they call just a friend.
The name is the same,
But they have reversed the game.
Girl I wanted to be your everything your all and all,
But I guess in the end,
I was just another midnight booty call.

(C S E A) Don't Pay.

Young brother's before you think about coming up, or pulling up,
Or riding up on that pretty young thing, you better wrap it up,
Or zip it up, because if you have not heard, then let me tell you about
C.S.E.A, they don't play and they will take your life away.
Brothers don't mess with child support because they will take every right you thought you had.
They will ruin your credit, they will take all your money, they will take your
Right to drive, and then to add insult to injury, put your poor black a** in jail.
Brother if you don't want to listen to old school,
Because I was use as a fool.
Believe me they've got all the power and CSEA rules.
Brother if you don't listen to me, then you will listen to CSEA,
Because brother they don't play,
Young brother I'm hear to tell,
They will make your life a living hell.
And the next thing you know you will be right here with me in the county jail.

When I Die?

Who's going to cry when I die? Who's going to mourn for me?

Will the world even notice that I don't live here any more, or will they just

Change the locks on my door?

Who's going to cry for me when I am not here any more?

Maybe they will put a new sign on my door saying he

Don't live here any more

And who's going to check the mail?

Who's going to forward my bills to my new home! Or will they even notice that I'm gone

--Just trying to make some since out of my life in a satirical way
June 2005

Cleveland

A beautiful city built on honor and pride,
But now politicians and greed,
Has Cleveland on the other side
As a kid I would love to ride the bus downtown, do you remember that too?
Now I've grown up there is nothing to do.
I can remember outside we could play,
but now it's not safe today.
Oh what has made Cleveland this way?
I can remember everyone on my street shared and had jobs.
Now everyone's fatherless and out for themselves and act like snobs.
I often dream of a better place,
But in reality is there such a place?
I've thought about throwing in the rope,
But my heart said nope.
Beside where will I go because Cleveland is all I know.
I dream that the politicians and greed would be put aside.
And Cleveland would be restored back to its glory days of honor and pride.

—June 2005

If the Walls could Talk?

If walls could talk, they would tell the story of an innocent little girl.

Her body was used like a piece of wood, and his penetration were like burning nails.

They would tell the story of an innocent child's living hell.

They would tell how she stays up all night and weep and weep,

So emotionally distraught, that she afraid to sleep

They would tell how she walks around every day living a lie,

And how her innocent soul wants to die

The walls would tell how she cried out, "no more, no more,"

But he continued as her innocent head hit the hard wood floor.

If the walls could talk they would tell how her assailant who she knew,

But was never caught,

Now she has to live this shame and guilt as if it was her fault.

Oh, if these walls could talk they would tell the tragic story of an innocent child living hell.

—May 2005

12Th Street

I 've worked my entire life but I'm still poor,
And now I have to make daily decisions whether to buy medicine,
Or food from the store
My job is not fair,
Because I'm living worse now than when I was on welfare,
But at least then I had health care.
The sky rocketing prices of gas and heat,
Has forced me to beg for food on 12th Street.
How and where can I live off of 150 dollars a week?
When all the money goes to the Child Enforcement Elite?.
Struggling between poverty and the child support elite,
I have been forced to live on 12th street.
I'm trying to get back on my feet,
So I don't have to beg for food on 12th Street.

My life has changed it seems like only yesterday when I earned 40 grand a year
My life really good and filled with cheer
Then the transformation transpired,
And I was soon fired.
No, no, not fired, but downsized.
Now I'm looked upon by society as the undesired
The company I once worked for is now in a foreign land
And now I find myself living on 12th street with a cup in my hand
I will not allow 12th Street to become my defeat and I'm going to remain strong, because I know that this designed poverty in America is evil and wrong.

—*I was asked to speak at the Truth Commission on poverty in America.*

You say you love me

You say you love me, and I know you're a winner.

But every time I've asked you out, you never have time for me or dinner.

You say you love me and that you care,

but when I ask to come over to the house you say "sorry but I'm doing my hair."

I've called to invite you to that new restaurant called the Loft

I've called the house and your cell phone, but like always it was off.

I don't want to whine,

but don't love require spending some time?

Well I guess I'll go home alone with just me and my pen.

And write about this love hurting pain again..........

Dreams Die

My teacher told me that I could not fly,

So I folded my wings and allowed my dreams to die.

When I was an innocent child, I believed that I could fly,

But my teacher told me, don't even try,

My wounded wings folded and allowed my dreams to die.

(2006)

We Ain't Got Time

We put our children name to shame
Because we don't have time for them
We're too busy seeking social fame
And trying to act like them because
We ain't got time
Our precious babies are crying at our feet,
But we sooth them with television
Rap, B.E.T. and M. T.V. are making their decisions
Parents we're acting confused,
Because we have allowed our children to be
used by this negative media tool,
And allowing others to discipline and make the rules.
Now you got little Ray Ray bragging on how he's pimping a hoe
While hanging out in front of the Arab store.
And Big John is talking about killing his own brother,
Because he sold crack to their mother
Look like we are never going to learn to love one another
And act like sisters and brothers,
Because we ain't got time
Parents we don't have time to teach them about their motherland,
Because our babies need to understand the importance of that,
But we can find time to buy crack.
Parents on Friday and Saturday everybody in the club getting crunk
Waking up the next morning with a hangover and still drunk.
Parents it is time to teach our girls how to act like a lady,
and our boys how to act like a man
So that they can be all that they can
As parents we need to put positive things on our children minds
Instead of partying all the time
Lexus asked her mother to buy her a math book.
Mom replied, "I ain't got time,
Because mommy needs new clothes, and designer pocket book."
Now ten years later little Lexus is all grown up, and she's hooked,

and she spends her hard earned money on
designer clothes and pocket books.
Parents we ain't got time, to develop our precious children minds.
Now little Ray Ray and Big John are both in jail,
Not because of the system
But because as parents we have failed
Parents we got time to do everything else,
But when it comes to our precious children
We put their hopes and dreams on a shelf.
We need to give our children praise and glory,
Before they end up on the back page of the
obituary as just another story
Here we are again standing on street corners holding up candles
and putting teddy bears on poles and building ghetto shrine,
When we should have be spending quality time
Parents let's find the time to cultivate our precious children mind,
And stop telling them,
We ain't got time!

My Room

I sit here in this darken little room, that now has become my very existence.
I did not for see this 664mile journey for knowledge,
Would bring me to Benedict College.
I close my eyes and recite the words of Dorothy in the Wizard of Oz.
I wish I was back home, but nothing happen, so I realize I must remain strong.
And complete this journey for all my ancestors who were done wrong.
I opened my eyes to overcome this stupid fear,
realizing that this is my destiny.
And it was God who brought me here.
This is sacred land where my ancestors shed blood, and many of them died.
I should be defending their pride, but instead to run and hide.
Here I sit in my darken little square room,
Acting as if my life is doomed.
This is the same place where my ancestors suffered, and were denied and education.
Yeah, this place is for black elevation,
Benedict College is here to show unification.
And build the minds of the next generation.
I'm feeling sad, and lonely,
I must reflect on the suffering of my ancestors,
and how they were treated so wrong.
I'm going to turn this light back on and keep on keeping on.
And until I graduate,
This is my home.

–

February Black

February is the month we all suppose to come together,
But some of us are still acting fair weather.
We talk about how proud we are, but we still ain't come but so far.
February is the month when the preachers and leaders talk about
How they marched with Dr. Martin L. King.
Only later to discover that those proclaimed leaders were the same people trying
To kill the dream.
February is the time to hear eloquent speeches with empty solution,
But nobody is talking about an economic revolution
Carter G. Woodson wasn't talking about televised programs,
he was creating a psychological renaissance,
So that the knowledge of self to can be taken to another realm
But instead were trying to act like them.
Well, I'm here to say that I ain't a February black.
I'm everyday black because my skin and society tells me that.
I'm that James Brown black because I'm saying it loud.
And I'm black and I'm proud.
I'm that brother you will never hear about,
Because I ain't selling out.
I'm that Marcus Garvey, who tried to set us free,
But some of some of us don't see.
I'm that Shaka Zulu, Cripus Attucks, Harriet Tubman,
Ida B.Well, Nat Turner, John Brown, Stevie Wonder.
Dick Gregory, Malcolm X, James Brown, Asa Hilliard
Haki R. Madhubuti, just to name a few that is true.
I'm that brother who goes to work every day to feed his family.
Working from payday to payday,
Striving to make it through another day
Those February blacks ain't willing to die,

But they are willing to comply
While they continue to preach,
and teach that white lie.
I ain't no February black,
I'm 365 days black
Because every day I awake my skin tells me that,
I ain't no February black!

To My Daughter

To my daughter daddy loves you, and daddy's love for you will always be true.
Because whatever storms life may bring to you, always remember daddy will be
There to see you through.
My daughter, I want you to love and respect yourself. Don't give your precious
Body to any guy because, if he's not willing to wait then tell him bye bye.
Tell him you're to smart to fall for that lie.
Take your special gift and store it on a shelf, even if you have to save it for yourself.
I will work any 9 to 5 if that's what it take for us to survive.
I will flip burgers at Burger King, if that is what it will take for you to be a true
African Queen.
To my daughter, loving yourself is to respect your self.
And to respect yourself is to love yourself.
My daughter learn to love yourself before you can love somebody else.
My daughter if life ever becomes too much for you to bear.
Please come talk to daddy, because I will listen to what you have to share.
To my daughter daddy is not going anywhere,
And I will always be there.

-I don't know how many ways I can tell you I love.
Terri I love you immensely.

Nigga Nigga Nigga

Who is a nigga and what is a nigga?
Well it has been said that a nigga is a fool.
Here is a list of nigga things, if you can relate to one or more of
These things on this list, then you just might be a nigga:

1) Nigga will spend more money then he earns.
2) Nigga will buy a cell phone just to call his own home
3) A nigga will dress to impress, before taking their money to invest.
4) A nigga sends their kids to a school that will teach them how to act like a niggas fool.
5) A nigga thinks getting a degree and a suburban address makes them free.
6) A nigga is a person who can build institutions to right the wrongs, but instead they build million dollar homes just so they can live alone.
7) A nigga will use the cliché "get yours like I got mines".
8) A nigga loves and accept everything and everybody, except his own kind.
9) A nigga is a person who doesn't produce or create anything for himself.
10) A nigga is a person who is always saying how it is much better than it use to be.
11) A nigga is a person who believes someone else has their best interest in mind.
12) A nigga believes the laws in America, is a symbol of equality.

—If you are interested in getting de-niggarized, de-niggerized niggas are standing by.
2006

Convicted of First Degree Murder

This was not your normal typical murder of revenge or hate.
No, this was a murder more gruesome,
Than any malicious murder of one's most evil thought.
This was a murder of love that was never meant to be.
The love she had most men would literally die for,
This love was too much for him to bear.
He would not allow her piercing love to manifest his stone cold heart
Her love was like the rays bouncing off the earth,
But it could not penetrate his heart.
He remained in this one sided loveless relationship only because of her unwavering love.
He felt bound and obligated to stay because of her love.
Many times he would seek help from the powers above to release him from her unshakable love. He desired freedom from this lopsided love, because it was causing him to lose himself in her love.
He knew that he could never return the love that his beautiful woman gave him so freely.
He told her the truth, but in her eyes it became an awful sin because she never wanted this lopsided relationship to end .It has been preached over and over again, how a woman will respect the honesty of a man. I am a witness that things do not always turn out as planned.
My honesty opened a blazing fire of pain, in the sake of releasing my own shame.
He couldn't remain in a one sided loveless relationship.
She did the only thing that she was comfortable with,
And that was to murder the thoughts of ever loving again.
She drowned her love by never loving again.
Two years later her love was found dead of a broken heart,
And he was convicted in court of love for murder in the first degree

2006

King James

He brought glory and fame to the city known for its shame,
This city has gone insane with King James
He made history by beating Detroit and going all the way to the title game
The city has relinquished their power and gave it to King James
His ability to ooze and oz the fans,
and literally has grown from a boy to a man,
in front of millions of fans
Let give him a clapping hand
Cleveland unified for this title chase,
and it wasn't about class or race.
James has so much game; the powers to be gave him a new name,
And called him the King James,
A title never bestowed to a player so young,
because of the game he loves to play for fun
He has brought people from all walks of life together
They all came the rich and poor
so they can witness what the Akron king on the basketball floor.
The King has dominion on his court, taking flight with great might,
shooting the ball with his left or right.
Oh! What an amazing sight.
King James has come down from his thrown,
and using his thrown to make our people and Cleveland strong.
He came to the inner city to unite,
and it don't matter if you Black or white.
The king is so smooth,
He is making MLK moves.

—June 2007

Goodbye

A part of me will die, when that day comes and you tell me goodbye

But I guess we're born to die,

And every day we live I die.

I wish I knew why?

And when I think about having to say goodbye,

My soul cry.

I truly believe with every death there is life,

And with every ending there is a new beginning

The day I met you my life began to transform,

Loving you became my norm.

It was like the caterpillar turning into a butterfly.

You made me look at the world in a different light,

And now quick as it began, it has to end.

I wish I knew why

I will not be able to watch movies with you late nights.

And we can't even be friends.

Saying goodbye sometimes just ain't right,

But we both knew it had to end,

So goodbye friend.

America

Why nobody ever told me that we ain't free and why ain't nobody ever told me who I'se be, and dat emancipation proclamation didn't set me free.
Why nobody ever tell me about that dare Fourth of July?
Why I'd wait until I'se grown to fine out something was wrong.
That, dare fourth of de lie was da white man's lie.
Now I'm grown I've figured some things out on my own.
Why in school white kids had their own rules?
I was taught that we suppose to sit on the back of the bus.
I'se sho thank that Mrs. Rosa Parks for putting up such a fuss.
I was told that America is the land of liberty and just us, then why they always
building all these prisons just for us.
Why ain't nobody tell me my history wasn't true, and that they kept
Books and wealth from people like me and you.
I didn't learn till I'se grown that that's Spaniard, Christopher Columbus in 1492,
Didn't sail no ocean blue, and most what I was taught wasn't true.
Why was I taught that, cause I'se black I'se better stay back?
And white was always right or they will come get me in the dark of the night.
Now I'se grown, I know why I wasn't in their history book.
Because it was my history that they took; so why would they put it in a book?
I just want to know why nobody ever said, it was ok to be black.
Well, it don't matter what nobody say,
cause I'se going to surely die black anyway.

Three Brothers and a Mother

My life, sometimes feel like an empty shell, because I never had an opportunity
to get to know my three brothers very well.
I wish I had known that they were never coming home.
I would have cherished every awaken moment we shared alone,
and assured them how much I really cared.

How I wish I could tell George, Ervin, and Jim.
How much I love them and miss them.
First it was my three brothers, then my loving mother, and I thank God that I
was able to recover.
I feel like I was done wrong,
because God took them before I was grown.
I know God has a plan for every man,
but damn there's some things I just didn't understand as a young man.
Sometimes I wonder had I not lost my three brothers and my mother
Would I have turn out like all the others?
But I'm glad that I am able to write about the personal
Things in my life are now right,
but I'm finally able to sleep at night.
This poem is for my Mother and Three Brothers
Sometimes I don't know what to do,
because of their loving memories
I'm some how able to make it through

"Sweet Memories"
—July 19, 2007

The Moments

The moments we shared are all mine, and it can never be advanced or reversed by time.

What ever happened yesterday and what ever will happen tomorrow.

All I know is this moment is mine, how do we, or better yet, how can we define time?

I will simply breathe in and exhale my moments with you, because these special moments are few. I don't know if this is real love, so I'll leave that up to the time makers up above.

As an earthly soul, my moments will never grow old, because my moments are persevered in gold. Moments are not defined in the past, present, or future.

My moments are moments stored up in the memories of my mind.

I don't know where life journeys are going to take me, but I've got my memories of you.

I don't know if the memories of today will bring happiness or sorrow, because

In the moment there are no tomorrows. –Just the Moments-.

-

July 23, 2007

Life

I woke up this morning and what did I see?

I saw life staring right back at me.

Will I face life today? Will I blame everyone?

For everything that has gone wrong?

Or will I fight and stay strong.

Love You

I Love you/ Will I love you today/ will I love you tomorrow?

My love for you will not change/

like the season change.

My love for you will always remain the same.

—2007

Hard to love Two

It is hard to love two, and my life is in constant struggle.

Because I don't know what to do,

I think my brain is going insane from this love game.

I know it's not right trying to love two.

I'm always hurting one or the other,

And claiming my love to be true.

I need to ask God what to do,

because it is humanly impossible to love two.

Two may be good for a pair of shoes,

But it's no good when you're trying to love two,

Especially if that two includes you.

-- October 11, 2006

Silent Tears

Dad forgive me for all the pain that I have burden you with

But most of all, forgive me for the many nights that you

have cried those silent tears.

Mom forgive me for not fulfilling your expectations, and hurting

You during my drug addiction, but most of all forgive me for

The many nights you have cried those silent tears.

Forgive me my precious daughter for not being there. To show

You how much I care, but most of all forgive me for the

Many nights you have cried those silent tears.

Forgive me for every woman that I ever hurt, because of my

Womanizing, but most of all forgive me for the many nights

You had to cry those silent tears.

Silent tears are those tears, too heart wrenching to cry out loud

These tears are cried alone. Silent tears are the tears that

Are cried in the dark of the night, when the heart and mind are one.

Please forgive me for those silent Tears.

-2007

Talk with God

God I have lied, stolen, fornicated, and cheated on my wife.

God I ain't been able to sleep at night, because my soul know

I ain't living right to make it to the top. I want to change my wrong to right.

I thought I was having fun but, I have to right my wrongs that I've done.

God, this I must share, because I'm lonely, depressed, and in despair.

God I do not know how much more of this life I can bear.

Oh, God, the way I've treated my beautiful wife. I am contemplating on taking my own life.

God replied,

"Son I gave you life to live in abundance, and not waste it on selfish pride.

I knew you even before you knew yourself. Some of your strife was ordered by me. In order for you to see, and now I'm going to set your soul free.

Now come on home back to me, and take that gun out of your hand.

It's time for you to become that God fearing man.

Son go talk to your God loving wife, she will understand her man.

Now go as I ordered, and speak with your wife,

and end this foolishness about taking your own life.

--

Arnold Shurn

Groove line

All aboard......all aboard

Hey, have you heard about this new dance craze that has hit the south?

Well, if you have not heart, let me tell you what it's all about.

This dance craze has gotten people from all walks of life to come together

And it doesn't matter if you are young or old.

The Southern Groove line is good for your soul.

However, keep in mind you will be traveling and meeting new faces,

And your destination will be many wonderful places.

And did I mention the southern Groove line is good for your health

So take those old shoes off the shelf, but most importantly do something

Good for yourself.

Now that you have heard about the southern Groove line, grab yourself a ticket

And come aboard. Now is the time to improve your health and meet new

friends because on this ride the fun never ends.

-

Happy Father's Day

Mothers are sweet, but Dads are unique.

Dad it is the little things you do, like when you showed me how to tie my shoe.

Dad it is the big things too, like going to work

Everyday to make sure I had clothes on my

Back and shoes on my feet, and a warm place

to sleep and food to eat.

Dad your strong love is always there even

When no one seems to care and life obstacles

Became too much for me to bear.

Dad you have shown me that hard work and

Dedication is the key for building a solid foundation.

Dad you are one of a kind, and I thank God that

He made you mine.

Dad I love you for always being there

—Happy father's day poem
June 14, 2004

Mayor Jackson

Mayor Jackson come out, come out. What is this really about?
Mayor Jackson the city need for you to come out. Have you heard or are you a sleep? Our children are dying in the streets.
I don't want to make this about black and white, but these killing
Of our children is just not right.
Mayor if these children were white
Would we see them on television every night?
Mayor, what's up with your police? They are never around.
Is it because they are too busy protecting downtown?
And when they do come around, they want to beat or shoot us down.
Mayor if they were white would we hear about them dying on the city street at night?
The answer would be no, because the Mayor, Congress, and the President would make it their fight. They would make sure the privilege whites made it home safely every night.

Why do black on black crime even exist?
It is because of this systematic self-destruction, and lack of job opportunities in the streets.
Mayor Jackson, it's time for us to meet.
Mayor Jackson come out and speak on our babies dying in your streets.
The Iraq war is right here on Cleveland's streets.
Mayor Jackson I just want us to meet, so we can stop our children from dying on the street.

--The mayor seems to have taken a hand off approach to the violence in the streets. The mayor has let us down, because all he care about is downtown.
July 2007

Blackman Suicide

Why do black men commit suicide? Because he is on the destructive cycle searching for success,
A success that never seems to arrive,
Because, he can't survive working that 9 to 5
He has never been able to obtain any clout, so now he's in doubt, about what his life purpose is about.
The black man is in a constant psychological strife, because, no matter what he does it is never enough for the rulers of this society or his wife.
The only refuge that he has is his home, however, that do not last long once his wife comes home.
She complains that, "you should be successful like my boss." A man's home is supposed to be his castle, but for him it's a hassle. To have this elusive success, he will sacrifice at any cost. He will even attempt to emulate his wife boss.
The black man is like any other man, he want to protect his family and fulfill his wife's desires. He chases that mad man dream of material riches and bling bling.
After while, he realizes that he's on a dummy mission and that this ain't his dream.
And that this shit don't mean nothing.
Brother's, life is hard out there, especially for a black man, and I do understand the struggles of the black man. Brotha don't stop being all you can.
Brotha it's time to stop chasing everybody else dream.
It is time to chase your own dream and find out what your life mean.
Brotha I know the struggles and strife of trying to live a dignified life.
Brotha taking the life that God and your ancestors gave you just ain't right.
Brotha put down that knife and live this miracle called life.

—Written 2003
Revised August 6, 2004

Greyhound

Greyhound is not the best way to get around, because the bus stops in every damn town.

And when you finally arrive at your destination, your body and mind is broke down.

Some people are really nice, and would try to help. But some people are just mean and are out for themselves.

The spacing on the bus is tight, and some people really smell. I thought I died and went to hell. Greyhound says, "Leave the driving to us," but I rather not because, it ends in discuss, whenever I ride that greyhound bus.

Sometimes the driver is disrespectful to us, and all I wanted was to get off that damn bus.

The food at the terminals taste stale, that food should be illegal to sell.

I've had better food in the county jail.

The prices are so high you have to ask yourself why? The food is not free and the prices are so high you will need the bank roll of Jay-Z.

Try riding that bus, you'll see.

Greyhound's famous slogan, "Leave the driving to us", forget all of that, how about giving my money and letting me off this damn bus.

—July 31, 2007

Daddy

Daddy, I called, but I got no answer. I thought I had dialed the wrong number,
So I called again, but still no answer.
Daddy where were you for the last 18yrs of my life.
Daddy I want to tell you that I've beat the odds and I'm in college.
Daddy I've got so many unanswered questions for you,
Like do I have any other sisters and brothers, and what happened with you and my mother?
Was I the blame that you never knew my name?
You never took the time to come to any of my football games.
Daddy I never told anybody this, but sometimes I would cry
When other children talked about the things they did with their daddy.
Daddy I didn't need riches or fame, I just wanted to
Ride home with you after my football games
And maybe stop and have an ice cream on the way.
Dad I didn't need to see you everyday,
But of course that would have been nice
However, I know that would have been
Too much for you to sacrifice,
Dad I'm 18 now, and after all that.
I have said; I still need you to be my dad.

—*August 14, 2007*

Angry Black Man

Society says I don't have a right to be angry, because I have my civil liberties, freedom and the right to pursue happiness in this America. Are you talking about the same freedoms to be followed and killed by people who are sworn in to serve and protect?
But the only thing I've seen is hostility, institutional control and total disrespect.
They tell me to get over my anger and that I'm living in the past.
Yet my people have not gotten what was promised to us.
We are still considered the poor under class.

This government can kiss my black a**. Our puppet leaders talk about reparation with a quiet hush. Yet no one in the senate or congress has come forward to put up a fuss.
You know what? Maybe Michael Jackson was right, they don't really care about us.
We need to wake up out of this dream, and stop walking around with someone else's name on our ass, bragging about how much we've paid for a pair of jeans.
Wake up, brother because, that shit don't mean a thing, we talk about how we want a piece of the American dream, but we keep killing our own kind for that bling bling,
That's keeping us blind.
Here's the real deal, we're accepted as long as we're playing on their basketball courts, smiling and entertaining or playing on their football fields.
We need to stop chasing the American dream, and start owning our own teams
We need to wake up out of this zombie state of mind, and then we can hire our own kind.
Well, it's just a thought. I'm was trying to awaken the consciousness of our minds.

Did you know this land was built from the sweat of the brotha man?
and I still can't get the bank and lend a helping hand
You have the audacity to accuse me of being an angry black man.
But it was you who left mass destruction all over this land.
You're trying to use this reverse psychology on me, by calling me anti-American and racist, because I want my people to have self- knowledge.
You rather see me in jail than in college.
We are still disenfranchised,
but one day soon we will realize.

I Can

I can because I can.

I can be what ever I want to be, because I can.

I can be a college graduate, because I can.

I can be the best person I can, because I can.

I can be a good father, because I can.

I can be a good mother, because I can.

I can be a good child, because I can.

I can be nothing at all, because I can.

I can be a drug addict, because I can.

I can change the world, because I can.

I can vote, because I can.

I can be all things through "God", because he said I can.

Yes I can,

Because I can

And you can too.

The Hall of Fame

Girl, I don't want to just bang that pussy. I want to make love and make you feel like you have died and went to heaven up above. I want to lick and dick your body.

And like Star Trek, I'll take you where no man has ever gone before.

I'll go Jamaican on you girl and make you sweat till you can sweat no more.

I'm not going to make your heart skip a beat, but I'll make it stop, then I'll gladly resuscitate you back to life with my caramel pulsating man hood.

I'll make that pussy dance to the beat of my bang, bang, bang, and girl you will be calling me all kinds of names. After I'm finished with that pussy, you will need a psychiatrist, because you will be temporary insane.

The fucking that I put on you will have me inducted into the Fucking Hall of Fame

Having achieved such great notoriety, I'll taste your sweet, sweet nectar and like a bee,

I'll suck the honey out of your honeycomb hide out and my tongue would form its own route. Guaranteeing special delivery and that's without a doubt.

Girl I'll have you shivering, curling your toes, pulling out your hair, speaking in tongues, and calling out Jesus' name. This is only a sample of why I was voted into the Fucking Hall of Fame. So before you step to me, you better know that I don't play no fucking games.

Since you think fucking is a game, then let's play twister because I am going to fuck you in every unimaginable position, and when I'm through you will resemble a professional contortionist. Now that I've beaten that pussy down in such a good way,

You will be expecting the Hall of Famer to put that fucking on you the same way everyday.

Girl once I give you this dick to ride, you will forget all about your boyfriend and push him to the side. In just one day the Hall of Fame fucker has gotten rid of that sucker.

Now that there are no more interruptions, I'll act like Mt. Saint Helen, and have you coming like a volcano eruptions.

Then I'll drink that hot pussy flow until you holler, "Hall of Famer, I can't take it no more." And if you ever in the area go visit the fucking Hall of Fame because you can still hear her calling out my name.

—Written by Arnold Shurn 2006

Home cooked meal

Young ladies today just don't cook, because they are to busy buying designer clothes and name brand pocketbooks. I just want a woman who can cook.

Young ladies today have lost their historical connection of cooking a healthy hearty mean for their family. Today's generation of ladies are too busy going nowhere fast.

The fast food chains has chained and bound this microwave generation of instant foods.

—2007

Skeet's

Skeet's is the place where you can come after a hard day of work and listen to some live jazz or have a bite to eat. You can put those rumors to rest because Eddie Bascus Jr. and Skeet's place it's the best.

Yes people come from miles around just to let their hair down, and to hear jamming Janice spin those funky beats. Now listen you can't walk in off the street.

So if your sagging or got your hat on backwards, we got K-Rock and Jerome Romie Rome to send you're a** back home.

I can recall way back, when this place was called Tim's. I do believe most of you old timers can remember him. Skeet could have let this place fall by the way side; instead he kept a leveled head, and had a vision to keep this place alive.

Now here I am at Skeet's at the Thursday night Gong Show. I'm standing on stage in front of these fine honeys's trying to beat the competitors so I can win me some money.

—2003

I wrote this while sitting at Skeet's night club, I frequently visit this place and that night they were having a gong show and I wrote this poem and performed it.

Love what does it mean?

Love what does that word mean? I've discovered that love is overrated, underrated, over used and abused. When I say I love you, do I mean it forever or will it fade like a pair of Levi jeans washed too many times in the washing machine.

Love is like a new suit, we wear it proudly when it's new, but after a few wears we act like its not there. Love is over joyous, love makes me glad, love makes me sad, but most times love leaves me loveless. Love is overrated; love is underrated, over used and often abused.

I will love you today, but will I love you tomorrow? Or will it fade like a pair of Levi jeans washed to many times in the washing machine.

Well I don't know but I do know that I will love you with all my heart, and if it does fade away, then at least I had the opportunity to love you for today.

—2002

Black is Beauty

Saturday night I witnessed an amazing sight.
It was like I saw the eight wonder of the world,
which could only be a creation by God.
I saw blackness in its pure beauty,
and I felt the power that it held.
This black was no ordinary black,
it was rainbow black, African purple black,
Vanilla chocolate black, caramel smooth black, black on black,
and that oh so good natural black.
I never felt the power of blackness.
I never knew blackness until that Saturday night at the Hush.
This black came in beautiful curvaceous lines, long legged lines, short powerful lines,
lines that had beautiful behinds,
and lines that captivated my mind,
These lines would be and artist dream to paint.
This black came in an array shapes and sizes,
pint size, medium size, big bone size
and tall model size
God must have sculptured these magnitudes of blackness
I was truly astonished with their beautiful forms
grape shapes, apple bottoms, melons, and triple D's.
These wonderful shapes were so shapely,
it all most made my shape change shape
Brothers you will never know the power of blackness,
until you experience Hush on a Saturday night.

—September 2, 2007
I don't believe the black queens understand how beautiful they are.
They don't need superficial enhancements to make them beautiful,
because they are the personification of beauty.
God is the artist and the black woman is his greatest masterpiece.
Thank you God for the black woman!

You ain't feeling me

You have allowed me free reign to discover every nook and cranny of your body, I've made love to you in every imaginable and unimaginable position. I've discovered parts of your body that you didn't know existed.

There is a part of your anatomy that you wouldn't allow me to explore, and that was your chained up heart. I guess that would have taken something much more. Girl trying to get to your heart was like kicking down a 20 inch steel door.

We made love, but wasn't in love.

We used each other private parts like divers use spring boards.

We bounced up and down and never really made that perfect landing via the heart.

We used our private parts instead of our hearts.

—2006

New Generation

The new generation they say we don't care, and I think this is so unfair especially when it was your generation who put us in this state of despair. Yeah many from your, generation have claimed to have marched with Martin and was there for Civil Rights.

But we didn't get in this condition overnight. Your generation settled for the right to sit on the front of the bus, and after that, they stopped fighting for the rest of us.

Your generation got them to change the Rules and allowed us to attend their schools, but today we are acting like nigga' fools.

Your generation loss sight, because they thought that everything was all right after gaining our so-called Civil Rights. Yeah, maybe my generation should have continued the fight, but we got caught up with the bling, bling and all those other material things.

We got tired of your generation talking about Martin L. King. How bout us fighting for our own dreams?

Our generation kept telling us that we had to work 3 times harder. And be 5 times smarter. So that we don't fail, but in reality all I see are 60% of black men in jail.

I do think our generation fail, because, we have got 60% of black men in jail.

Your generation worked hard to get jobs, houses, businesses, and land, but somehow that too ended up in somebody else's hand. Your generation gave up the fight and started drinking, partying and smoking dope at night.

Here we are today, the new generation as a result of your success, we are crack babies,

Crack heads, crack dealers, and now we done cracked up.

This new generation that I inherited is so fucked (messed) up.

Whoever the blame for this generation, we have to unite the old and new to change the situation.

—*October 2007*

Jena 6

It started with a noose hung from a tree, and that was seen through the eyes of some as a mere joke. Well its and evil joke when they can take the lives of 6 young men, just because this Reed Walter want to impress his friends.

Like a junkie shooting dope, I think this D.A. is getting his fix, but he didn't plan on all of America getting in his mix. I think this D.A. wants to see how far his sick thinking can go. But he didn't figure on black people standing up against this injustice.

Here shouting "no more and D.A. Walter has to go." The buzz around town got people talking. What are they marching for? They got their freedom after the Civil War, so they shouldn't be fighting any more.

Well, in the words of Martin L. King, "injustice anywhere is an injustice everywhere," and that is why we are marching on Jena 6, because it ain't fair to keep them there, and that is injustice everywhere.

Fannie Lore Hammer said, "She was sick and tired of being sick and tired." I'm sick and tired of these KKK officials for hire. People stop acting like we are free and open our eyes to see. All we got to do is turn on their television, and you will see injustice bestowed upon people just like me.

No my people we ain't free, because we have to inject something in our minds other that MTV and BET. There are a lot of things in this country that need to be fixed, so we are starting with Jena 6.

People, let's fight injustice support the Jena 6, and get in the mix.

September 2007

~After going to Jena 6, I had to write something about this blatant disregard for human rights. This D.A. Walter Reed is displaying to the world his true colors.

The government of America has given their message, that black life ain't got any value. I'm just wondering when we will stop being ignorant and annoying the fact that we need to pick up the torch for our own damn freedom~

Lost Innocence

Life in the box called the hood where little children have become hard, cold, and insensitive towards death. They play in crack infested streets where dead bodies replace the chalk lines that were once used to play games like hopscotch.

They play in playgrounds plagued with HIV dope needles, and bullets that rains out like rain falling from the sky. I witness these atrocities and I ask God why?

How have these innocent souls become so harden toward death, as if it was a natural inheritance . They have learned to weather the storm and bullets shots in the hood is the norm. They don't even flitch when the bullets ring out through out the hood.

Their young conversations are not of the lessons of school, but of the harden lives that they have lived in such a brief time on this earth known as the hood. Where every thing in their existences is of no good, and that just the way it is in the hood. Little Tommy tell his dreams of reaching the age of 25. These are the dreams they dream in the hood instead of these precious gifts from god dreaming of becoming doctors, lawyers, and scientist. They dream of growing old at the ripe age of 25.

These innocent souls have witness more deaths than a soldier at war; because where they live they are casualties of war in a war zone commonly known as the hood. Their misconception of life is standing in front of abandon buildings claiming their hoods. Killing each other over land which they have no deeds to, because they got nothing better to do.

Their forced to live with this exterior toughness from what they've witness in movies and videos. Now they are disrespecting women and calling them hoes. Because TV has taken the place of parenting because mommy is working two jobs and daddy is in jail for selling dope. And because of him the entire family is in disarray, hanging on by a thin rope.

The world has passed them by, because every time you turn on the TV, what do you see? Well, you see them talking about wars and hunger or how they've sent millions of dollars towards humanity for the sake of good, but those same innocent children are still dying in the hood.

What happen to the days when kids were able to play in the hood, because it was all good in the hood as we over stood? Back then you could look out from your windows and see the future of hope. Kids would be out side riding their bikes; girls playing hopscotch; boys running to see who could run like Jessie Owens or Carl Lewis. Back then we played hard and had lots of fun, because we knew when the streets lights came on we were done.

The street lights today represent dead bodies and chalk lines of lives that once lived in the hood. God I ask just one thing, can you make the hood all good so that these innocent souls can have the life they should?

—"Peace"
Just a little bit of love is all we need. 2007 the Messenger

"PAIN"

If I could take your pain and change its name, I would.

If I could take all my love and heal your pain, I would.

If I could make your darkness turn into light, I would.

If I could find the right words to comfort your broken

Heart, I would.

Life's experiences have shown me that pain won't last for always.

If I could take your pain away just for a moment, or for a day, I even wish I could make it go away, I would.

Since I can't make your pain go away, I simply will say I love you today.

Young Men come Home

Young men are going to war and no one knows what for.

Young men are being used as body shields because Bush wants more oil fields

Young men are dying for a lie and the American people are standing by

Young men are coming home in pieces, and some can not walk because we have a president who does not know how to talk.

Young men over there are brave and they do care, but back home their families are struggling and on welfare. Young men Bush said he was going to give you the equipment to fight this war, but can't you see that you don't need no 60 million dollar embassy.

Bush said that you're fighting to make this country safe and strong, but these same young men can't get adequate health care back home.

This Bush administration does not care about these young men welfare, because if he did they wouldn't be over there. Young men how are you making America safe from terrorist attacks by fighting a war in Iraq? Is this Bush guy drunk, or is he getting high on his own crack? Young men I commend you for fighting this war, but I still do not know what you're over there for. Perhaps I could understand; if these young men were fighting in Darfur.

Bush stop this personal war, because it is costing us in health care, education, and making us a third world nation. We need to spend the taxpayers' money on universal health education, and to fight discrimination. This would restore us back to glory and pride as the number one nation.

Bush it is time to bring these young men home because you know in your heart of stone that your personal war is wrong.

Just trying to shine some light onto a senseless war, because I just do not understand what these young men are dying for in seven year war

2008-

Voluminous Ass

I saw you walking pass with that voluminous ass, and you always smell good, looking good; damn I bet you even taste good.

I wish I was the one holding you tight on those cold winter nights. I wish I was the one soothing you, rubbing your body down with oil or putting strawberries and whip cream on your groove thing.

You're the women that I have always desired because you have all the attributes that I like: intelligence, respect for yourself, and lots of class. Last but not least, to complement that class you have a voluminous ass.

You Fuck Me and Fucked Him Too

You fuck him, you fucked me, and fucked him too.

Now I don't know what to do, because I was in love with you.

I know you're not willing to get rid of the other two, but at least tell me what to do.

Because I have fallen in love with you, but you can't keep all three so who is it going to be?

What is this?

America tragedy, traumatic experience, medical treatment, vote, Iraq, shelters, schools, education, lost homes, abandon hope,abandon dreams, abandon lives,- helplessness, homeless, hopeless, lower ninth, deception, distraught, distress, disaster, devastation, negligence, government, FEMA, poor, unequal, sad, mad, hate, horror, pain, more pain, death, more death, help, no help, relief help, Red Cross, Mental illness, Army, guns, third world, levee's, Action, motive, food, water, babies, transportation, helicopter,
Kanye West, Bush, disenchant, disease, disgust, New Orleans, Rise Again, Illiterate, licentious, race, God, economics.
Never forget!

It Ain't About Me and You

I'll take some of the responsibility for our hopelessness.

But some of the blame is on you too, it's not all my fault that your life has been reduced to looking out of the window of what could have been.

You are mad at every man that crosses your path, because of the choices you made.

It took two to make three and now you're mad at me. Had we known that fifteen minutes of oh baby, ah baby this is the best I've had; would lead to a life of pain and hate towards one another. Now we hate on each other like two steps brothers born from separate mothers.

We're only focusing on two, and that is me and you.

We have fallen into this self-destruction behavior of it's all about me.

We need to open up our eyes to see that it ain't about you and me, but the number three. We got to realize our wrongs and make them right, so we both can sleep at night.

Because we hurt each other when we fight and act wild; when we should be thinking of our child.

Yeah, I know I said that I'll never leave and that I'll always love you,

Bull Shit

Every time I look around there's always some bullshit. And it doesn't matter if it was a hundred years ago or twenty years ago or today it's the same old shit bullshit. And everybody thinks their bullshit is more important than the next person bullshit, but no matter how you look at it, it's still bullshit.

Yeah I know everyone got bullshit in their closet but I wish that people would keep there bullshit out of my bullshit and keep their bullshit to themselves.

It do not matter who shit it is, because it could be mishit, their shit or whomever shit it's still bullshit People always talking about this shit that shit and I'm tired of everybody's shit; even my shit. Every since the beginning of time the bullshit been going on ad people are still bullshitting, but remember you can't bullshit a bullshitter.

And while you are sitting here thinking about this poem. You'll finally realize this poem is full of bullshit.

OBAMA

We need to alleviate this blame game and stop this drama and rock the vote for Obama, and In order to restore hope we need to utilize our vote.

We don't need no old man McCain he'll make us all in insane and drive this country further in the drain.

Vote Obama and not McCain if you really want real change

Brothers

Black on black crime isn't it time for us to stop getting angry and losing our minds,

Just to kill our own kind.

For some senseless, I don't know why I did crime.

Brothers we have enough obstacles in our way,

Without having to worry if we're going to be kill by a so called brother today.

Brothers do you realize that we're walking the same walk and running the same race,

it's not about what yours or what mines,

We must stop with this killing of our own kind.

We must do away with this black on black crime,

Because brothers I don't have a dime,

And I go to work just to get mine.

And it's no longer the Jim Crow laws or being lynched from a tree,

Because death today comes by the way of a brother who looks just like me.

Brothers killing brother's every day,

And we got to find a positive solution,

because this ain't the way.

We got stop this envy, disrespect and strife.

What we need to do is focus on living a more productive life.

We got to stop polluting our brothers and sister with all this dope,

Give them a future and a ray of hope.

Brothers it is time for us to come to the table of brotherly love,

So we can show one another that it takes respect sharing and love,

To uplift each other after all you are all my brothers.

~I wrote this to shed some light on the senseless violence of gangs in the projects. Our young boys and men were fighting over territory that they had no deeds to, and selling drugs to survive and making the drug cartels and the United States & the Prison Industrial Complex rich, while families buried the children physically and mentally.~ When will it end?

Tears I cry

Oh, the tears I cry when I see my people struggling to get by.

Oh, the tears that I cry for the state of mind of my people. Oh, the tears I cry for babies having babies, and babies without fathers and fathers without fathers. Oh, the tears I cry for the racism that cripples and strangles the mind of my people.

Oh, the tears that I cry for the modern day slavery disguised as justice. Oh, the tears that I cry for the institutionalizing of my brothers and sisters. Oh, the tears that I cry for self–destruction of my people.

Oh, the tears that I cry for the lack of self-knowledge; instead of my young brothers standing on the street corners they should be in college seeking knowledge.

Oh, the tears that I cry for the lack of leadership in my community or shall I say our community. Oh, tears that I cry for the banking institutions that takes, takes, takes and gives nothing in return but false hope things to be desired.

Oh, my tears of thee the land of modern day slavery.

Oh, the tears that I cry when I see my young brothers with their heads down in despair like they just don't care. They have lost hope and now they are standing on the corner selling dope.

Oh, the tears I cry when I see my young sister prostituting their minds body and soul and for what? For a brother standing on the street corners with a neck full of gold, that stuff is getting old it is time for the real story to be told. How we produce the fruit of this land and yet as I stand I am still considered 3/5 of a man.

Oh, these are the tears that I cry for the state of mind of my people.

A.A

Time after, time after time I thought I was on the verge of losing my mind, because I was hanging out with my so called friends on the street corners and drinking beer and wine.

Waking up two decades later, only to realize I've wasted valuable time and time is like money once you spend it you can never get it back. Today I no longer have to be miserable and suffer like that.

I'm grateful to my higher power for showing me a better way, and that way is A.A

This wonderful organization has no dues or fees, and I'm allowed to be me. A.A has not only taught me how to stop my stinking thinking, but how to live without drinking.

Albert Einstein said, "Insanity is doing the same thing over and over again and expecting a different results."

Today I 'm doing things different and getting different results,

and those results are living peaceful, happy, joyful and free. Just for the day I'm living life again the A. A. way.

Life does get better one day at a time, so try the A.A; it will restore your mind, and you won't have to wake up twenty years later wondering what happen to your time.

Arnold Shurn

Confederate Flag

Here we go again, complaining about the Confederate Flag in 2010. We can show the world that South Carolina's does have class, by getting rid of our dark evil past. By starting with taking the Confederate flag down, off of the State Capital grounds.

South Carolina's we can make a change, because it never too late. This horrible flag represent a time when America was not so great. America itself were terrorist and acted insane, but to allow the Confederate Flag to represent all South Carolina's is a crying shame, and it gives us a bad name.

I'm sure African Americans are elated that the Industrialized North won; if not Negros would probably still be working in the hot sun. Some have said they've earn this right because the South put up a good fight. This may be true, so this is what I suggest they do: the few, who still think like them, take your ideology and your Confederate flag and build yourselves, with your money a museum.
The Civil War ended in 1985; however, it has been kept alive with the representation of the Confederate Flag. Today is Martin L. King birthday, a man who has represented peace and love, yet the Confederate Flag is still allowed to fly high up above.

HERE WE ARE AGAIN IN 2010, SEEKING TO GET RID OF SOUTH CAROLINA'S PAST SINS.

"WE THE PEOPLE OF SOUTH CAROLINA WANT TO FORM A MORE PERFECT UNION, WE DECLARE THAT THE CONFEDERATE FLAG BE REMOVED FROM THE PEOPLES STATE GROUNDS."

TAKE THE CONFEDERATE FLAG DOWN!
Arnold Shurn

Fancy Cell Phones

Why do people talk on their phone so long, especially when they just left that person two minutes ago at home? And why do people talk on their cell phones at the intersection, while trying to make a left turn; after the light has changed. I think these telephones possess evil powers, and are driving people insane.

And tell why do people have to have an hour text conversation on their phones? Are they conscious that texting is dangerous? It only talks a blink of an eye to kill themselves or someone else, while texting on their fancy phones. Why can't they wait until they get home?

That important conversation will not be so important when you are dead and gone.

Please stop texting on your cell phone, because it dead wrong. Many tragic stories have been told, yet people are still wiling to give up their lives and souls. When all they had to do, is do the right thing, and pull to the side of the road.

I guess that conversation is as good as gold, because you are willing to risk your chances of ever growing old.

Talking and texting while driving is a horrific sin, and I strongly disapprove of people who play by their own set of rules. Talking and texting is a human sin, because it killed my best friend.

People we don't need a law to tell you that talking and texting is wrong. Next time you find the need text to just remember that my best friend never made it home.

Feb 21, 2010
A .S.

Pull Your Pants Up

The cliché, "I wear the pants in this house, and I am not afraid of another man, because I put my pants on just like him."

During that era it symbolized responsibility, authority, and courage.

However, today representation of how a man wears his pants has a different connotation. Now it is about this distorted representation of building a reputation, with this new generation.

I've begged them please, but they still wear their pants below their knees. They say, "man this is sag." I tried to explain to them that style originated from prison, and it represented that you were a fag.

Furthermore, I explained the historical context of saggin: saggin is niggas spelled backwards, and was a tactic for slave master to keep niggas dehumanized.

Nevertheless, they go on about their merry way, so I guess their saying it is cool to be that way. Well, why stop there, if you're going to wear your pants below your knees?

You might as well put your butt up in the air, and wave it like just don't care because obviously you want another man to stare.

Real men don't sag, so pull your pants up on your waist, and stop this human disgrace.

Young men show some class, and stop acting like you want another man to put some dick up your axx.

> *~I wrote this because I am not judging because all generations had their thing. I am trying to inform and give some context to originality of that style. And allow them the freedom of choice to make an educated and informed decision~*
>
> *The Messenger. Feb, 2016*

I Dialed my Brother Number

I wanted to call my brother to tell him how I was feeling about life, like we always do and just to chant a few. I called his home but no one was home. I said, let me make sure I got the right number, so I redialed 277-4444, and there was silence and then a voice low and sweet said, "He's no longer at this number, but this is how you can get in touch with this person with this number."

"You have to call his new number direct, and that number is 244-7777." "That number is the direct line to heaven." So, I dialed the number as instructed, and an angelic voice answered. "Who would you like to speak to?" "I would like to speak to my brother because I have not spoken with him in a while." "What is your brother name?"

"His name Miss is Jerome Romie Romie. The voice on the other end began to laugh. "What wrong Miss?" "Nothing." Yes,we definitely know Romie Romie. I know who you want. Let me go get him off the dance floor, He's up here doing a dance off to More Bounce to the Ounce.

Hello, bro. "What happening?" I just wanted to tell you I miss you." "I'm fine." "Man it was just my time." I'm absent from the body bro but still present in your spirit and mind. "Tell everyone, I am fine, and that they will see me again on God's time, so keep me near in your spirits and minds."

"Rome I miss you man our conversations, when I was weak you would encourage me to stay strong, and you would tell me to hold on even if I had to hold on with one hand, but just don't let go." "You would tell be to stay strong and just do the best you can, because you are a strong black man."

"Tell everyone I love them, and I know they don't understand but it was all ready written and now I am in God's hand. Everyone will be fine in due time; when they realize my time was never mines, and that I was just living on borrowed time." Tell my family to live life like there's no tomorrow and wipe their tears away, because I have no more sorrows and I don't have no more worries about tomorrow. "I will continue to pray and watch over you guys, and when God come for you, I'll save a dance for you too.

"Okay, bro you got my new number call me anytime." I am out of sight but never out of mind, so when you need to talk just dial my new number. Tell family and friends I love them and I look forward to seeing them again. Peace out! Later, I got to go spin, and I love you to the end.

Love you brother ... to infinity!
2015, Nov

Valentine is all the Time

Andressa we don't need no Valentine to define,
I love you not just on this day,
But all the time.
Valentine is just another way,
Because I don't need a specific day to show you how I feel every day.
I don't need Valentine day to give you a treat,
Because I show you every day
From the top of your head to the bottom of your feet,
I am not going anywhere, because I am here to stay
Valentine Day should be a special day about just us two,
I don't need to show the world,
Because this about me and you,
And you already know I love you girl.
Yes, I love you, so I'll do whatever you want me to do,
But remember this is not about a day.
When Valentine is through,
guess what? I won't stop loving you.
When the candy and roses are gone
I love you every day,
because there's no other way.
I will still be making our house a home
I don't want you to think just because I buy you things.
That my love only represents material things,
I whether give you everlasting memories of happiness,
Our time together is much more precious than that diamond ring,
I just want us to stay together, because our love is strong enough to face the good time, and the bad times,
so I don't need no Valentine as long as your mines.
You set my heart on fire, all I want to do
Is give to you the joy that your sweet heart desire?
I want you to remember when Valentine has gone and passed,

Our love for each other will last.
I love you all the time,
So don't get caught up with this man made Valentine,
Because I love you and you will always be my Valentine.
SO WILL YOU BE MY VALENTINE?
Written 2/14/18 to my boo, I love you!

Love Dangerous Highway

If Love is a two way street, Why am I always going down a one-way street, the wrong street, dead ends, and slippery roads. I'm always riding with my windows down looking for the right road to travel that will get me there with the lease amount of effort.

The directions are clear and the roads are clear, but my vision becomes blurred and I want to take the short cuts, and I turn down the road that says DO NOT ENTER.

This road seems familiar, because I've travelled it before. I take the detour again looking for a quick fix to find love.

The road ahead becomes a little cloudy, and as I continue there's a blizzard. That blizzard becomes a storm. Instead of me turning around, and taking direction I continue to drive in the storm, which seems to have become my norm.

I take my chances, because that what I do.

The road are dangerous and unsafe, but I make it out alive.

This time, I made out safe, but I can't keep taking these dangerous curves expecting to survive.

Love is a dangerous Highway, and I can't keep driving recklessly down Love's dangerous Highway.

Michael Dunn & his Gun

Here we go again trying to justify the White man sins. This Michael Dunn character went too far shooting ten times inside those teenage car, all they was doing was playing there music and having fun. Here comes Mr. White privilege with his gun.

Mr. Jordan did not deserve to get shot down, and now the cold blooded murder want to use this his white privileged Florida law call Stand Your Ground.

This Stand your Ground Law is the modern day lynching. What law is next? Hang a Nigga from a Tree Law. Legalizing hanging black people from a tree, and through my black eyes this is what I see.

A black child can't play his music loud, he can't wear a hoody, he can't wear his hat back, all because he is threatening to the White man' Stand your Ground Act

Every time the White man shoots us, we are not allowed to defend us, because under their law it is called justice.

We Pray! We March! We Vote! But they still use they their legal Rope!

Black Code laws, Voting laws, Vagrancy laws, and these laws were not equitable or fair, because white man laws don't apply to us, so do not go there.

The Stand Your Ground Law has to be removed off the books, because it only benefits the rich White crooks. Don't believe me look at the innocent Brown and Black lives this law has already took.

American people let's get real because if we don't white men will continue to hide behind their laws that allow him to kill base on how he feel.

I am talking to the American People of all races, creed, and gender it is time to make this stand your ground surrender.

How many more innocent children will be killed, murdered, and shot down, before the people decide to stand their ground? Now's the time to stand our ground because parents are tired of burying their children six feet underground, because of this unjust law called STAND YOUR GROUND.

Let's tear down the Stand Your Ground!

~This law was created to help white people who felt like their lives are being threatened by an aggressive person, and they have no other options but to stand their ground. What if this law was fair across cultural lines? I as a Black American felt the white man was a threat and was the aggressor, and I feared for me and my family life, and I put one center mass to the head. WOULD the Law STAND ITS GROUND for a BLACKMAN? CAN I get equal Justice under the law? IS Lady Justice Color blind to BLACK and can only been seen when the WHITEMAN waves his mean GREEN? ~

Trayvon Martin

Trayvon Martin didn't have to die, and now the entire country want to know why?
Wearing a hoodie and carry a bag of skittles, that could have been anyone of our sons.
And yet here in this land of the free, we are still waiting for justices to be done.
Hoodie, skittles, and ice tea gives you the right to kill me.
Where is justices and that lady liberty for me?

Hoodie, skittles, and ice tea that could have been you or me.
I wonder if the Black man really free!
Cause this a common occurrence for a Black man like me.
That racist Zimmerman killed a child half his weight,
And making the claim that his fat ass was protecting and guarding their private estate,
And that Trayvon should not have been visiting his father inside their private gates.
The Stanford Police are now indecisive, and want a debate.

Well, I say the Stanford Police are out of touch with the
human race and that can't relate.
We stand today in support of Trayvon Martin and his family,
And maybe this injustice will bring unity to a broken people and community.
Zimmerman a coward, who has the law and a gun in his hand,
and now Trayvon Martin will never grow up to be all that he can or become a man,
because of a racist vigilante who has the law and a gun in his hand.
This coward walk away uncontested and despite the outrage this animal is not in a cage.
We stand today for justice, and we stand for want is right.
The racist media stop making it about Black and White.

Look in your heartless hearts and do want is right.
Trayvon Martin is you and me,
American it is time to take the blind fold off of injustice,
So Justice can see,
Because Trayvon Martin is you and me.

~ Fact: Did you know this child Trayvon Martin was in studying do be a Pilot? ~
Arnold Shurn March 24, 2012
Finley Park Dirty South
@ Third eye Poetry

MY LAST HOUR

The last hour of my life, I want music playing, poets' readings, and people dancing.

I want my last moment to be a representation of living, because that is want I did. I want love spreading like seeds of a good harvest. My life is in the last hour is not death but life that moved on to the light of life where you must transcend to another realm of understanding.

My last hour will not be a representation of sorrow, but the every lasting transcending memory of tomorrows. With darkness comes light and with light comes darkness. Death is like night and day I can't have one without the other.

I want my last hour to be my finest to tell the real story of my journey called life, and tell the story of my final destination as the best and most honest as I can so don't sugar coat it, because I know there were some uncomfortable missteps, and some mistakes along this journey called life, but as a child of the most high, there is no need for me to be lying or you all crying.

So leave those boxes of tissues at home, and men you can leave those three in the pack handkerchiefs' you have stored away on the left side of the dresser draw beside all those pills you taken at home.

This is not a crying festival, if you want to cry, and then cry before you get there. I don't have no more pain, I don't have to fight against injustices anymore, because I fought long and hard, and I did my best. Now let me get some rest.

Now play my favorite song by my favorite artist, and get this home celebration started.

`Later, my friends and family I've done all I can as a man, and I fought my best fight, and ran the only race I knew how, now it all over and it is time to cross the finish line~ Just know I love you and keep me in mind sometimes~

Libya Where Are The Crys For You?

aMERICA WHERE ARE YOU? IS IT BECAUSE MY SKIN DON'T REMIND YOU OF aMERICA, or is it because my skin is Black, Purple, Blue, and it reminds aMERICA of you? America LIBYA cries for you, they are asking how can you aMERICA not see my beautiful Blackness from the land of the FREE.

Does LIBYA remind you of the terrible history, when Rosa Park refuse to sit on the back of the bus. How can you let this happen to us? America help us, by calling your senators, Congressmen and your President. Nobody is listening, Nobody putting up a fuss, maybe this America don't give a dam about us!

America where are you with your influence, moneys, battleships, and big guns?

Maybe you can't see me, because you are blinded by the sun. Where are you?

AMERICA LIBYA IS CRYING FOR YOU!

I Can Complain About

I can complain about,

I can talk about it,

I can complain about

I can do something about it,

I can do nothing about it

I can do something about it,

I can do nothing about it,

I can complain about

"Far too many people are waiting for the next person to do something, and nothing ever gets done, so we end up complaining."
~2012~

Fear of the Truth

If the truth was told would you listen? Throughout America's history the White Supremacy has taken over the Black people history and put them in a state of perpetual fear. If we are truthful at examining the truth, the black people our being used as the stepping stone to enhance everyone else's quality of life. They have made the white man's generational wealth sustainable for centuries.

Black people will not accept the reality of their conditions that we have not gain freedom, and that we do not have the same privileges as other non-black groups. White and other non-black groups of people have not lifted themselves up by the boot straps. They had assistance by the Government the same government they claim to hate. They have been given millions of acres of **free** land, free labor, and subsidies to build their wealth, bank loans, and enormous other free things from the government.

When non-white people begin to ask for subsidies to get progress they are called lazy, and when they try to become self sufficient they are brought down or bombed or jailed for wanting to have a SHARE OF THE RESOURCES OF THIS LAND. They have given non-white people the deception that they have the same opportunity as anyone else if they work hard. I am here to tell you the truth is a lie.

There is a known secret; well, how is it a secret if it is known? Okay, you're right. Let's change that to there is a code that many of the so called successful people must adhere to by those that produced the monetary system that the world is subjected to maintain their existences on this planet. And anytime the Negro steps too far out of line they will destroy him financial or simply erase him. They are not allowed to invest in the dilapidated communities

For example: Michael Jackson was becoming too powerful and by owner 50% of Sony he had to be erased, Malcolm X tried to empower his people with freedom, and he was erased, Dr. King began to talk about going to Washington for our un-cashed check, and he was erased. To bring you update with a more recent annihilation of the successful Negros is Bill Cosby who has been a warrior for decades advocating for economic empowerment and freedom. He was in a position to buy NBC, and tried to purchase it along with other affluent Negros. Now you have all these allegations from thirty years ago, suddenly surface about him raping women with drugs. They are using him to let you Hollywood Negro's know that the money you got "ain't" got no power.

Finally, Black Negro, African American my friend needs our help he was fired from his state job for trying to help build a youth center by requesting funding to build a youth center for our children high poverty areas of South Carolina to decrease, and hopefully eradicate the school to prison pipeline.

THE American FLAG

The Red White and Blue mean something different for me and you,
As black man in America I have a different view,
The millions of black babies, women, and men who decided jump off the ship,
Because they chose death,
And not to be brutally whipped,
Just to create your wealth
Rather than live less than a man in a blood soiled land,
By the hands of the white man.
Red is for all my innocent Black people who died for their honor and pride,
And for the helpless mother who weep and cried
The America you saw was of hope and dreams that were full of stars,
My ocean blue of America was filled with the darkness at the bottom of ship
I could not see the stars, because I felt the bloody scars.
The America you see is the land of the free,
But lady injustices is blind she can't see .
In 1492, is not the true,
Because we had already sailed the ocean blue,
America's Independence day in 1776, they screamed freedom from their lips.
My freedom was an occasional bucket of water to clean the bows of the ships.
The American Red, White, and Blue,
just ain't the same for me and you.
You celebrated freedom drinking wine and having a good time,
But I am told to erase my history from my mind,
I on the other hand, as a Black man,
Had to muster up the spiritual power,

Because I was not allowed to shower
To overcome the rat infested darkness in the bottom of a ship
While you praise freedom from your lips,
Rats ate at my flesh at the bows of the ship
As you honor and celebrate your historical moment,
I had to endure the stint of defecation,
And regurgitation of a sick nation
Is America the land of the free?
Lady Justice needs an eye examination for glasses,
Because she dam sure can't see,
Because she can't see her justice ain't the same for her and me.
You sing the star spangle banner and wave the flag at me, while singing the land of the free.
You created the first amendment for the free, but a black man can't take a knee.
That lady justice needs to take that blindfold off, so she can see that the American flag don't represent the same thing for her and me. The police suppose to serve and protect, but I only receive total disrespect and neglect. When they come on my side of town, even when I hold my hands up, get on my knees, and I lay down. They still shoot the black man down.

We march and put up a fuss,
But the law makers don't care about us.
You talk about dying and going to hell,
Try being a black man in American working for free,
on this modern day plantation called jails.
The Red White and Blue it ain't the same for me and you.
In 1862, Homestead Act was for you, they gave you land as a White man,
And provided you a helping hand
The Homestead Act didn't help slaves,
Because they were still Black

We pledged the allegiance to your flag of the United States of America and to the republican in which it stands one nation under God individual liberty and justice for all, but that all have not kept its allegiance to all.
You painted the black man as a dangerous man, but you I killed millions while holding your second amendment rights guns in your hands. Today, you still don't respect the Blackman, because you want me to stand for a flag that celebrated slavery.
The star spangle banner, "No refuge could save the hireling and slave/
From the terror of flight or gloom of the grave"-
This is celebrating the deaths of slaves
You want to continue to dehumanize, demoralize me as man and make me stand.
I can't reverse time or erase the evils of America's sins,
But I can write the truth about America through the ink of my poetic pen.

~Dedicate this to Kaepernick---5/31/18
By taking a knee, he made a statement that we still ain't free from the injustice that permeates inequality and hate. Thanks for your bravery!~

"Big Mike"

Mike I promised my brothers, mother and countless others. I will take their deaths and live my life with more purpose, more determination to eradicate this spirit of self-hate. Marvin Gaye said, "Only love can conquer hate. My tribute to your life is to live life more purposefully, by using every single breath that God allows me to breathe. I will use it to inspire, to dream, and to motivate change.

Mike your time, your journey has an expiration date & yours have arrived. Yes, people we are here today to say our goodbyes, I don't want your tears to be hollow, I want you to fight with love for our precious babies, so that they can have a possible future for tomorrow. This mean community, civic organizations, churches, activist, and last but not least parent we must teach our girls how to act like a lady, and our boys how to act like a man, so that they can be all that they can.

Therefore, if you are here to honor my nephew, the only way to really honor "Big Mike," is to live your life, and do in your hearts what's right. We have to learn to love and put these guns down, because if we don't it won't just be Big Mike being buried in the ground, so please for the sake of our love ones put the guns down!

Too many mothers, sons, daughters, aunties, cousins, friends, uncles are having to return to their broken homes, and when they go to look in their photo books there are missing memories of what could have been, because their tomorrows never came. What we need is a thunderstorm of love to rain down in our war zones to bring a cease fire on this storm of self–hate and violence! If we our blessed to see another tomorrow, let's show more love by having more smiles; more hugs; more kisses; more gratitude and less attitude; more respect and less neglect; more hellos & less goodbyes. I am so tired of wiping tears from my eyes because another love one has died. Let's restore our people, our community back to honor and pride.

I am asking you do not walk out of here as if it's just another day at another funeral; it is time to reach into our pockets and pull out our moral compass. This community must recalibrate our moral compass to place that leads us to a destination called love, and once we find love, we can restore hope, and with hope we can have the unlimited possibilities for change! This is the only antidote that going to cure us from this of deep rooted mental illness of self–hate that is infesting our communities. The scripture says, in Ephesians 3:17, That Christ my dwell in our hearts by faith we must be rooted and grounded in love. I want to thank you all for your presence, I want to thank you for your now, but most of all I want to thank you for your love!

LOVE YOU MIKE … who was brutally murdered on E119th between Union & Kinsman by a murderer who used an AK-47 & shot 13 times

Written by Arnold Shurn on May 2, 2018

Brother I Miss You

Brothers 1,2,3, and now my brother 4 I will never see you again walking through my door, but now you're knock, knock, knocking on heaven door. I text you and you say you were going to call me back. Why you had to leave me this way, because there was so much more for us to do and say.

Now I got to speak loud so you can hear me way up above the clouds, bro you know that you were my road dog and best friend. I'm not going to question God why he wanted you end, but I just don't understand why he took my road dog and best friend.

The hopes and dreams we shared as men in our deepest moments, and just like I promised mom when she transitioned on her journey to the pearly gates. I'm not going to wait; I will spend every precious seconds of my life living and fulfilling my dreams. I am going to take life by the bull horn bro and live like my next breath is my last. I am no longer living my dream, I'm living it for my road dog my best friend. This dream is for two and that me and you.

Now cook outs will never be the same, I won't be able to hear you brag about being the grill master, and how you put everyone the shame with your cooking game. In your humorous way screaming Romie Romie in the house, Man I miss you! I'm not going to be able to get my free haircuts no more, so that mean I got pay a barber and that going to make my pockets sore; man I am going to miss you even more.

Who am I going to talk to about how fly we dress and those European cut suits?

I love you bro but I still think I am the best dress.

Bro, I love you but God got something better for you to do. He might want you up there to cut some hair or maybe tighten up the angels' wardrobe and teach them how to dress. (Here's an inside joke), God might want to taste the beef side of the ribs you be grilling.

I MISS YOU, but never will forget you because I'll be living the dream for me and you. I'll see you when I get there! Love you Romie Romie God as call you home.

Written: by Arnold Shurn: to my brother who left on a one way ticket in his name on God's train.

10/4/2015

Thanks Dad

Dad I want to apologize for being opinionated, and hollering out I am grown. When in reality I had no clue on how to make it on my own. You allowed me to make my missteps and stumbles, but through it all you never allowed me to fall.

During that time of my maturation I did not understand the process of becoming a man. Thanks dad for showing me that the definition of a man was not measured by the tool in my pants. I learned that a real man did not think below his waist, but above his shoulder.{And for you women out there allow them men to use those shoulders to carry some weight} Thanks dad for the plethora of memories you allowed me to store.

I remember the time you rented that camper when we stayed on Iowa, and took everybody out of town; I remember when you took us to the race track to see white people drive really fast, and I remember going horseback riding. Today because of the seed you planted, my wife and I want to acquire some land and get some horses donated to create a therapeutic environment for inner city children. That's want real men do, they plant seeds and cultivate them so that they can grow. You don't plant them and walk away from them.

Thanks Dad for having class, because the memories you've created will always last. You see memories will never die, because what you gave me I will with every breath that I breathe pass it on to my seeds and cultivate them; so they too may grow.

Thanks Dad for teaching me respect, because that is one thing that will never grow old. You see that thing called respect. You know that song Aretha Franklin sang about. Thanks Dad because I learned on my journey to becoming a man, that respect will take you places and open up doors that I would have never imagined. Thanks Dad for planting that seed. Thanks dad for being a man of contents and substances.

Thanks for being a man that I and others want to emulate. I got my work cut out for me, but if I could become only a portion of the man you are dad. My family, community and the world would be a better place.

Thanks dad for never having to go to bed hungry. Thanks dad for keeping clothes on my back, shoes on my feet and a warm place to sleep. Thanks for always being there, and your action showed that you care. I present this day for you to show my appreciation for all you do, so today I would like to create some memories for you store away.

Dad I love you for just being you, and making me a better man,
because of your example I know what it takes to be a man
Written by Arnold Shurn, July 4, 2014

If I could Change the World

Listen up Boy & Girls,

If I had the power to change the world,

I would bring love and peace, throughout the world, and the Middle East.

for all the innocent little boys and girls.

I would eliminate rich and poor,

with a wave of my hand it would be no more.

I would make education a fair game.

No more corridor of shame-

Only do what Right, and eliminate this illusion of Black and White

If I could change the world, that what I would do-

Make the world a better place for me and you!

Jan- 2012

Man I miss you

Brother 1, 2, 3, and now my brother 4 I will never see you again walking through my door, but now you're knock, knock, knocking on heaven door. I text you and you said you were going to call me back. Why you had to leave me this way, because bro I had so much more to say?

Now I got to speak loud so you can hear me high above the clouds, bro you know that you were my road dog & my best friend. I'm not going to question God why it had to end, but I don't understand why he had to take my road dog & my best friend.

The hopes and dreams we shared as men in our deepest moments, and just like I promised mom when she left for her journey to the pearly gates. I'm not going to wait; I will spend every precious seconds of life living & fulfilling my dreams. I am going to take life by the bull horns bro and live like my next breath will be my last. I am no longer living my dream, I'm living it for my road dog my best friend. This dream is for two & that's me and you.

Now cook outs will never be the same, I won't be able to hear you brag about being the grill master, and how you put everyone to shame. In your humorous way screaming Romie Romie in house. Man I miss you! I am not going to be able to get my free haircuts no more, so that mean I got to pay a barber and that's going make my pockets sore; man I'm going miss you even more. Who I'm going to talk to about how fly we dress, I Love you bro but I still think I'm the best dress.

Bro, I love you but God got something else for you do. He might want you up there to cut some hair or maybe tighten up the angels' wardrobe and teach them how to dress. (Here's an inside joke), God might want to taste the beef part of those pork ribs you be grilling.

I MISS YOU, but never will forget you because I'll be living the dream for me and you. I'll see you when I get there! Love you Romie Romie God has called you home.

Written: by Arnold Shurn: to my brother who left with a one way ticket in his name on God's train.

10/4/2015

You don't Know How I Feel

Your children are not housed in Urban warehouses prison preparatory schools of false education,

You don't know how I feel, because you don't struggle to pay your bills,

You don't know how I feel for real.

I see abandon buildings,

And abandon lives.

I see the rich exploiting the inner cities,

Oh what a shame, what a pity it just ain't fair in the inner city

I see other people walking away with their pot of gold,

While my people work their poor fingers to the bones, and wishing and praying that they can grow old.

You don't know how I feel.

God's Ultimate Glory is in my story-

The ink in this pin is like the blood, it helped deliverer me from my sins and God's words seem to overflow from within. Every time I pick up this pad and pen God's scriptures begins to flow within, and it gives me the strength to fight the temptations of sin.

Now instead of injecting dope; I'm injecting gods' word to offer others hope from their sin.

God shed his blood and died for the world sins, so that we can start all over again. I am not looking back on what I use to do, but what god going to used me to do.

As a poet I speak this spoken word, but the true poet is God's word. John 1:1 says, "In the beginning was the word and the word was with God, and the word was god."-

Church you do not know my troubles and you don't know my pain, once upon a time my life was insane because I was caught in this dope game, so one day I decided I no longer want to live this way. I told myself that I had to get right because if God came like a thief in the night and took my life, and I died in sin. Then ultimately the devil's eternal hell would be my end.

Saint's stop blaming the devil for our wrongs and start being obedient to his word and allow God's power to be the head of our community and our homes, and if we do that we can never go wrong.

To be conscious of sin and to continue to do it over and over and over again; is a dangerous game my friend, which will lead to God's ultimate judgment in the end.

"Through God I can do all things"

The First Dance

It was dark and people were dancing and having a funking good time, and from the other side of the room I saw a beam of light shining from a far.

I began to approach this creature of beauty, and it was as if God himself sculptured this tall slim midnight star.

It could have only been God himself to make something this magnificent to view for the human eye. She was a Goddess among the mist.

She had coca brown skin, voluminous lips that were made for someone special to kiss. I was to be so fortunate to be in her mist.

I mustered up enough courage to ask a goddess to dance.

She said yes, and man I felt blessed: though I only stood at her breast.

The sensation in her hand had the power of romance.

We danced a second dance, and I began to believe that I died and went to heaven. My heart skipped a beat and, I felt as if this goddess had swiped me off my feet.

After she privileged me with a second dance, I wanted so much to touch this blessing with my hand.

However, I knew I was just a mere mortal man, and it would be foolish of me to take that chance. She blessed me with a third dance, now I am confused and don't know what to do?

This can't be happening to me, it must be a dream, so this can't be true.

I need to calm my nerves, because I can't think.

I need a drink. Oh, but I don't drink.

Dancing with her felt like I ascended to heaven with this Black Goddess, I hope this dance never end because I want it to start over again so that the first dance is our last dance.

Written, by Arnold Shurn

December 12, 2012

The brother was at Green's in South Carolina, and I danced with this fine young lady. I was feeling her and she was feeling me but it was just not meant to be, because she was not totally free.

Advice Ain't Free It Cost

To my precious biological daughter and to all my spiritual daughters, I want to say **I love you, and I want you to sparkle and shine like the true diamonds you are.** When I provide you with advice it is by no means to belittle, dehumanize or make you feel less than. I want you to know that no one on this earth has the power to that, because you are a precious rare gift from God, and because of your God given status you are not above or beneath any human being. Therefore, you can hold you back straight and your head high, and know when you walk into a room, yourself confidences will radiate and illuminate mother earth.

When I provide suggestions don't look at me like I am speaking in tongues and you need and interpreter to comprehend. I give this advice not because I want to exert my authority upon you; I do because of my unwavering and unconditional agape love for you. Okay, here is my advice to you:

1. First stop telling me that I am not perfect. I know I am not perfect, but that do not give you an outlet not to strive to be the best you that you can be.
2. I do not want you to settle for things that are not good for you. I do not want you to make the same mistakes I did. I want you to love yourself, and when you learn to that, the people you allow in your life will know how to love you; because love is the core and it will radiant from your existence.
3. I want you to know thy self and love thyself and respect thy self.
4. Educate yourself through reading and taking good advice, because good advice is good for you.
5. Learn the value of a dollar and learn to save, and know the significance of credit.
6. I want you to be honorable women, and if you happen to make a misstep it only becomes a mistake if you repeat it again.
7. I want you to be careful when it comes to those slick leg guys that will whisper sweet nothings in your ear, and don't fall for

the baby I love you and I'll give you the world routine. Here is some good advice so pay attention to this? As a man first and a father second; let me shed some light on what a men really what from women. Men are natural hunters and we will say or do whatever it requires to have our way with you. And once we devour are prey, we are on to the next victims. Dogs will chase the cat. Once you give up that prize possession to someone who don't even know your full name or honor and respect you. You can never reverse the hands of time and take that moment back, so baby choose wisely the first time.

8. If you don't you may end up pregnant with no money, no education, and no emotion or financial support from that handsome boy who promise you the world, but only gave you a baby girl. A guy should have a plan for his life, because if he has a plan for his life, then he can make plans with you for a life.
9. Learn that happiness begins with you so learn to be happy, because for every second you are angry, you lose a minute of happiness.
10. Your mind is like a garden and your thoughts are like seeds, you can plant flowers or you can plant weeds (quote unknown).

I give you this advice because I have earned the right to provide you with this bit of value experience of information. First, and foremost advice ain't free. I paid for it with my years of pain and suffering. Just like God dead for our sins, so that we can have ever lasting life. Well my precious daughters, I have made the mistakes for you, so that you don't have to follow down that lonely road of self- destruction and shame. The decision you make today dictates your life.

Take this advice; because advice ain't free, and mistakes ain't free they will cost you. It's just one cost more than the other
Written by, Arnold Shurn
6/2/14

Letters: I written to attempt to make a change

Fatherless Fathers

The current child support law appears to be a replica of the Black Code Laws. These the laws were implemented in 1865, after the Civil War for the purpose of denying former slaves equal access to economic opportunity and financial freedom. In many states, if unemployed, blacks faced imprisonment. Apparently child support has taken a page out of history, because they can now take a man's driving license and lock him away in jail because he is unable to pay a debt to child support, and after he serves his time, the debt is not alleviated. Men are unjustly imprisoned not because they are not willing to pay, but because they do not have the ability financially to pay or the means. This is where the distinction of being a "dead beat" dad and a "dead broke" dad comes into play. Minorities and poor whites are unfairly targeted by this legalized extortion. There is an urgent need for a resolution to this critical issue, so that fathers can resume their God given natural roles as fathers to maintain the family structure as financial and emotional providers.

The father role is to provide for his child's emotional and financial need. However there are obstacles beyond his control. For example, government never implemented any programs for the indigent fathers into the family welfare reform program. The real concerns have never been addressed such as: being unskilled and undereducated in a school system that prepares poor children for prison and not well paying corporate American jobs.

Resulting into a myriad of people demanding, that the poor people needs to get better paying jobs, and stop being lazy and join mainstream society's 40/ 40 club. The 40/ 40 club is working 40 hours and 40 years. Unlike President Roosevelt during the Great Depression, he devised a plan; however, that plan did not include the black people, because of the nature of their employment, which was agriculture and domestic. Fast forward to today, the welfare plan unfortunately does not enhance the economically disadvantaged. Furthermore, these institutions continue to perpetuate the pernicious cycle that demoralizes the poor by legally taking money from those who least can afford it. Here is the overview of the current welfare system:

- Back child support
- Non-custodial parent assumes all economic responsibility for the custodial parent being on welfare
- Provide minimum wage jobs/ no medical coverage
- Separation of family/ creating Parent Alienation Syndrome
- Shift total poverty responsibility to the father

The welfare system falsely projected an image that the system was designed for the purpose of uplifting poor families out of their condition of poverty. This deception allowed generations of families to rely on a handouts rather than a way out. The welfare narcissist view claims that it was the indigent fathers' failure for not lifting his family from the depths of poverty. This institution was created for the purpose to luring a certain group of people into a false sense of security. The welfare system never offered or provided a viable training prior to the 1997, Reform Act.

This flawed system continues to mislead the public of their intentions by using the deception of smoke and mirrors to solve complex but simple problems.

This issue must be addressed. This is like trying to solve a bullet wound with a band aid. These poor families do not need more social pacifying programs. They need solution rather than jails and institutions. These fathers need an economic plan so that they can take care of their families like God planned, and not this Industrial Complex Prison plan. Amendments are urgently needed to alleviate this family crisis, because the current plans do not promote family; it promotes incarceration and disunity and family separation. This unjust system has distorted, twisted, deceived, and manipulated the ignorant public into believing that the poor father wants to shun his fatherly responsibilities. However, turning a blind eye on governmental policies relating to the poor, that affects fathers' inherited rights to be a functioning component in their children lives.

Here are suggestions that will alleviate this crisis and bring structure back into the families:

- Give indigent fathers an alternative to jail/community service to improve the plight of urban decay
- Make it mandatory that indigent fathers learn a marketable skill through the father initiative, grassroots programs, and churches
- Offer both parents emotional support, so that they can have a functioning relationship; if conditions allow
- Make it legal for the indigent fathers to claim their children on their tax return; if the mother is on the welfare system
- Amend hostile laws imposed on the indigent fathers: Taking their license; Eliminate potential earning clause law, which makes it extremely difficult to obtain a modification, the current law states that a person has the potential to earn what she/ he earned from previous job
- Volunteer to go the jail law/this law states that if an individual cannot pay due to loss of income or no income; then the person volunteers to go to jail

Amending these unjust laws will alleviate this legalized extortion called; "back pay" support, and help these poor fathers decrease their insurmountable debt. This too will motivate welfare recipients to break the vicious cycle of welfare programming. It is ironic that this law is called "back pay", when African descendants demanded back pay for their free labor that created the wealth in this great country. You could hear a pin drop in the halls of America moral consciousness towards humanity and justices. The silence was loud and clear to the sufferers of America's blind unbalanced justice. Have the Father's cries fallen on death ears?

Finally, this system if it wants to allow all Americans to live out their inalienable rights to have life, liberty and the pursuit of happiness. They must enact a just system that reinforces the family structure and less hostile towards the indigent family. The most important part of the equation is the children, whom have been used in this bureaucratic shuffle, and now they are left to swim upstream without a life jacket. Justice for the indigent father will come, when they decide to unite resonate voices to the masses for justices. It is apparent that our political leaders our political puppets who lack humanity, and are unwilling to jeopardize their careers for poor families and fathers. Fathers hear my cry! We can no longer sit in the stands as spectators and simply complain about the demise of our roles as fathers, and continue to accept the role as victim. Now is the time to display to our children that we are not spineless cowards, and we will fight for our natural God given right to be fathers to our children. Despite the inconceivable obstacles ahead, we must stop this legal but illegal business of profiting off of the pain and suffering of our families. We must not allow them to continue to dismantle the institution of our families.

A Father Cry-
Written By Arnold Shurn (2000)

Letter: to expose the shame and the pain to defame father's name

The Fathers Cry

Specifically, how does it benefit the children if the Child Support Enforcement Agency (CSEA) is imprisoning and revoking poor fathers' licenses because of their inept employment and economic deficiencies? How can the fathers become the back bone and the head of their household if CSEA's current laws are allowed to exist?

Legally and morally, fathers should have an opportunity to nurture, cultivate and support their children. Apparently, America's ideology of lifting yourself up by the boot straps has not trickled down to the poor fathers in America; thus making it more difficult for them to achieve economic success when their boots and their straps have been taken away. According to the 2000 census data, Cleveland State University researchers informed the Urban League that 345 of Cleveland's 242,481 African Americans live in poverty and about 46% of employable blacks are without jobs (Plain Dealer Dec 8, 2003). Fathers must unite and lift their voices to demand that CSEA offer something other than jail. They must demand gainful employment, psychological support, and that these current laws are amended.

Fathers pride themselves in being gainfully employed and taking care of their families. However, when money from gainful employment ceases to exist than that pride can dissipate rapidly. The lives of these poor fathers begin to regress and they find themselves in a crisis. In addition to their misfortune, they are confronted with the assassination of their character by being falsely labeled "dead beat dads" when in fact they are" dead broke dads." There is an obvious distinction between two.

Furthermore, it appears that CSEA's primary role is not to promote the welfare of the family, because if it was why not attempt to uplift these poor fathers so that they can have a positive impact on their families. Every statistic and data supports the significant impact of having the fathers in their children lives. Dr. Frances Cress Welsing, psychologist and author of *The Isis Paper, states, "Denial of full scale employment results in the demise of the Black males, because they are unable to adequately support themselves, their wives and their children" (V). The results are that a number of Black males' children grow up without their fathers' guidance. This leads to frustration, depression, and failure in the schools.*

Millions of children are fighting a courageous battle growing up in working poor families where the fathers are playing by the rules, however, cannot earn livable wages or receive adequate support from their government that will allow them to better themselves(Covenant xiv). Who will hear the silent cries of these fathers who want to escape from poverty but just do not have the resources? This constant uphill battle takes a toll on them psychologically and can become too much for them to bear. Psychologically, these fathers can become emotionally distraught when opportunities continue to evade them. Imagine the mental anguish these poor fathers endure by not being able to establish nurturing and loving relationship with their children. Equally important, who authorized CSEA the rights to constitute the role that these fathers can play in their children lives based solely on income. There is something evil lurking.

Children need psychological support from their fathers. Everything is not about measured by dollars and cents, but we need to take common sense approach. For instance, there are things such as producing life, teaching a child how to walk, ride a bike, tucking a child in bed and confirming there are no monsters under the bed. Most importantly, just being there to tell them that daddy" loves them," this has huge impact. These moments are invaluable in any child's life. There may be monster, but not under the bed. They are the people that are dividing, and making the monstrous decision to exclude fathers from their God given role has fathers.

Psychologically it would be more beneficial for the family structure if (CSEA) took a less hostile approach and prompted marriage. Marriage could be a possible way for stability. Specifically, it could

increase financial stability by having two parents earning an income. Secondly, the statistics for out of wedlock children would decrease drastically. The psychological benefits of having two parents in the home are immeasurable. This will eliminate the separation of families and the single mother syndrome, and this why there needs to be a sense of urgency to amend these unfair laws.

Child support Enforcement Agency laws need must be amended to restore the institution of family. Here is a list of some of the current laws that are not conducive to the family unity:

1. Revoking the indigent father's right to drive.
2. Current law being on welfare.
3. Separation of family
4. Fathers imprisoned for being poor or unable to pay

Here are some suggestions to alleviate and restore our families:

1. Allow fathers to drive if they are seeking gainful employment ; have jobs/attending school/medical emergencies
2. Make it legal for indigent fathers to claim their children on their income tax returns if the mothers are receiving welfare
3. Offer both parents psychological support so that they can heal the scars of dysfunctional relationships; if the conditions allow
4. Give indigent fathers alternative to jail/ community service in their neighborhoods to restore their community

Fathers are not requesting these amendments for the purpose of shunning their fatherly responsibilities, but because they want to be fathers to their children. Is that wrong of them?

Furthermore, who are the benefactors of fathers having their license revoked and placing them in prison? Certainly the children have not benefitted. These poor fathers desperately need these laws amended because the current laws do not promote family; they promote incarceration, destruction and disunity.

Finally, fathers cannot continued to bullied or succumb to this child support business that continue to deny them of their civil liberties, due to an institution based on economics conditions. Poor fathers have endured this continuous psychological attack from this new form of institutional slavery disguised as justice. Stop locking fathers in jail, because of their economic condition, and assist them with overcoming their conditions. The mighty Child Support Enforcement Agency should not be that Iron Gate to prison, but a gateway of opportunities. Fathers must lift their silenced voices and demand that CSEA provide gainful employment, psychological support, and amend these for profit bias laws. Fathers we must demand that our God give inheritance as father be restore back to its rightful owners, so that we can raise our children, and not allow these bogus laws to distract us from our purpose of manhood. This is our cry for support from community activist, churches, and all who wants to save our future generation from this bias system that is designed to keep father from their natural position as men. These man made laws are destroying the infrastructure of poor families and keeping fathers from their God given natural roles.

Wanted Real men and people who wants justice for all, and believe that these innocent children deserve a fair chance.
Contact: A Father Cry
shurn.arnold@yahoo.com
Facebook/ Arnold Shurn

Letters: To attempt to produce change for equality

Hi, and good evening to all those who are present

I would like to thank those who are responsible for bringing this forum to fruition.

My statements to the officers are? I do not want to put all police in the same category, because I have had some positive encounters with the police, and I have had negative experiences as well. With that being said, since I do not believe all police are insensitive to our communities. Nevertheless, I do believe all police should be held accountable for their actions, and should not be above the law. Policemen and policewomen if you see a fellow officer committed a violation and you turn a blind eye like that lady justice turns a blind eye on her unbalanced scales of justice you are as just as guilty. Do you remember when you were children and both of your siblings got caught doing something and the parent's law was if you did not tell who did it, you both got in trouble. You were guilty by association.

I know there are dangers in breaking the blue code of silence, but you are sworn to serve and protect not disrespect and neglect.

Secondly, I do believe with the recent and past data around the nation concerning the shooting of unarmed black men and women around this nation, that is the time for a conversation as to what is an just and unjust shooter and when is deadly force required.

I want to know the language that justify a white man to carry a gun, and why an unarmed black man is more dangerous than an armed white man who can kill hundreds of people in school shooters, and is arrested and allowed due process of the law, but the police do not allow black men and women the same due process. Therefore, I guess my question is what makes unarmed black men more dangerous than an armed white man with an assault rifle.

This makes our community go beyond suspicion, and I believe we have a valid reason to question the due process, because of the preponderance of evidence.

Personally, I believe there is something evil lurking within this criminal justices system, in which the administering of prison sentencing towards a certain population of people. This is where the correlation enters the equation with the prison industrial complex, from a business perspective they are profiting off the backs of our precious children.

Finally, I do not have to quote a plethora of statistics, because many of us here in this room are familiar with the disparities that are prevalent in our communities. I am sick of tired of being sick and tired of the police department around the world putting a band-aid on a bullet would, and brushing us off with eloquent speeches with empty solutions. The police must change their administrative investigation process where it is fair to the citizens that they claim to serve and protect. They need to stop policing our communities and become peace officers.

The administrative investigation is an insult to the victims. I want to reference the children analogy. Here is an example: Your parent when you were a child would catch you dead to the wrong, and there were disciplinary actions taken. You were told that, because you did wrong I am going to allow you to discipline yourself to correct your own behavior. That what an administrative investigation is, and the verdict is always the same not guilty in the eyes of the laws there were not reasonable or sound information discovered to find our officers in the wrong for murder or negligence on the behalf of our internal investigation.

Then there are unjust laws that allow white men to murder innocent black children under laws created by white men. We cannot change the hearts of the heartless/ and or the hate that is inside another human being, but we can change the laws of this land. We will no longer sit by and remain silent and do nothing to protect our babies. We have allowed our children to shot, and buried six feet underground by your castle laws and your stand your ground.

Hands Up Don't Shoot! We are standing our Ground!

Thanks, Peace be with you

People often look outside of their community to find heroes, just because a person is not on television or radio do not take away from their contribution to humanity. I want to recognize my dear friend and a man I respect to the utmost.

Here is a letter I wrote to the Tom Journey Morning Show:

Reach Media, Inc
Attention to: real Fathers Real Men,
1370 Noel Road Suite 750,
Dallas, Texas 75240

Arnold Shurn
Address info: exclude
February 21, 2014

Frank a Man of integrity and Character

I want to begin by thanking Tom Joyner for providing an outlet that allows black men to dispel the negative myths concerning their roles as men. I would like to nominate Mr. Frank Washington for the REAL FATHERS REAL MEN AWARD, because he epitomize what this award symbolize.

I have known Frank for over forty years, and he has always represented a genuine spirit of love as a father, husband, brother and real friend. He has been with his lovely wife for over twenty years, and raised his children with that old school moral and values that many of us who are over forty was accustomed to, so one might question what so exceptional about that, because that was the norm during that time? Yes, you are absolutely correct so let's get straight to the point.

This is what makes my friend Frank worthy of this award:

Frank has started something that has taken on a life of its own, and has become a tradition for the men in our community. It began with a simple desire to get a few friends and family members together on father's day, to have a good old neighborhood cook out. This event of brotherly gathering has come to fruition for now nineteen years. Frank's brother Jessie has fallen gravely ill, who has been in attendance since day one of this annual father day event.

Unfortunately, Jessie had a stroke and was diagnosed with diabetes, which resulted in the amputation of his leg. Frank took his brother in and is taking care of him, and has allowed a lifelong friend to move in who has fallen on hard times. He is doing all this while maintaining a job, and assuming his role as a husband, father, brother, and a friend. Frank is what REAL MEN and REAL FATHERS exemplify and he is a man that other men want to pattern their lives after. Men like Frank do not come around too often, a man who is willing to give unconditional love by giving of his finances, self, and time.

Tom Joyner will you please help Frank with this year expenses and make it really special this year for Jessie. I want to honor Frank's good will and dedication by eliminating the financial burdens, by asking Tom Joyner show to provide food for about 50- men, T-shirts and a banner. This will relieve some of the work load off Frank and allow us to be a blessing to him, since he has been a blessing to us for so many years and to so many people.

Contact info: Frank Washington
Address excluded for the purpose of book

Sincerely,
Arnold Shurn

Bio: Mr. Arnold Shurn

I was born and raised in Cleveland, Ohio. I attended Forest Hill Parkway Elementary, Patrick Henry, Margret Spellacy Hamilton Jr. High and John Adams High School. I graduated from Cuyahoga Community College with an Associate Degree in Liberal Arts. I obtained my Bachelor Degree in Interdisciplinary Studies at Benedict College in South Carolina. I went on to obtain a Master at South University in Mental Health Professional Counseling. I served honorably in the U.S. Army.

Speech written during my candidacy for Councilman:

I am a Community activist & public servant, so don't get me confused with the political rhetoric I am that person who is unafraid and unapologetic when it comes to addressing the core concerns of our community. I am fighting to reverse the mental psychosis of a hopeless people who have been: criminalized, demoralized, marginalized, dehumanized, and it is time for us to wake up and realize we on the verge of genocide.

I want this community to know that I hear your silent voices, and I see your tears of hopelessness. "I know change is often an uncomfortable transition, but it is also a necessary transition. "My priority is to continue to support the grassroots," organizers and like minded people who are committed to making our communities a safe& decent place to live. I know the heart piercing pain of these senseless acts of violence, because I lost three brothers and a nephew to these senseless acts of violence.

We can no longer sit on the sideline, as mere spectators. I do not want another family to experience the pain of losing a love one prematurely to be robbed of their future memories.

Secondly, we have to address poverty with something applicable, which can be measured. We have a Banking and Political System, intentionally engineering poverty to maintain this criminal infestation in our communities. Their only interest is to promote their private prisons systems, and the inner cities are the commodity.

The mechanism to produce wealth in the inner cities has ignored communities that look like yours and mines for far too long, and reduced our opportunities to become self- sufficient. Those of us who are gallantly fighting for equality for our communities are often left in the shadows alone, and our tremendous sacrifices are unseen. Now is the time to resurrect our dilapidated communities and make them a decent and safe place to live. However, this will not come to fruition if only a few continue to carrying this heavy load of an entire community on their backs. We got to stop ignoring the problems, as if they are going to magically disappear, and until the people of this community acknowledge the elephant in the room called violence. There will be no measurable changes. The people will continue to hear politicians come in their communities around election time and give nothing but eloquent speech with empty solutions. It is time well over due, that we must recalibrate our moral compass in a direction that leads us to a place called love. If we can restore love, all the other ailments that are plaguing our communities will vanish. The scripture says in "Ephesians 3:17, 'That Christ may dwell in your hearts by faith that we must be rooted and grounded in love". "Now is the time to resonate our voice, so it can be heard all way down town up town& all around town. Let's resonate our voices so loud that it shakes the foundation of City Hall and Washington D.C.

STOP VOTING FOR A NAME! STOP VOTING FOR THE SAME! VOTE FOR ARNOLD SHURN IF YOU WANT REAL CHANGE!

Thank you. Peace & One Love!
Written by, Arnold Shurn

Printed in the United States
By Bookmasters